It's another star from the CGP galaxy...

Here's the thing: you can't cut corners when it comes to Grade 9-1 GCSE Physics. You really have to practise until you're 100% confident about every topic.

That's where this indispensable CGP book comes in. It's bursting with questions just like the ones you'll face in the real exams, including those tricky required practicals.

And since you'll be tested on a wide range of topics in the real exams, we've also included a section of mixed questions to keep you on your toes!

CGP — still the best! ☺

Our sole aim here at CGP is to produce the highest quality books — carefully written, immaculately presented and dangerously close to being funny.

Then we work our socks off to get them out to you — at the cheapest possible prices.

Contents

☑ Use the tick boxes to check off the topics you've completed.

Published by CGP

Editors:
Jane Ellingham, Robin Flello, Emily Garrett, Rachael Marshall, Jonathan Wray.

With thanks to Glenn Rogers, Frances Rooney and Ian Francis for the proofreading.

With thanks to Ana Pungartnik for the copyright research.
Graph to show trend in atmospheric CO_2 concentration and global temperature on page 98 based on data by EPICA Community Members 2004 and Siegenthaler et al 2005.

ISBN: 978 1 78294 517 8

Clipart from Corel®
Printed by Elanders Ltd, Newcastle upon Tyne

Based on the classic CGP style created by Richard Parsons.

How to Use This Book

- Hold the book <u>upright</u>, approximately <u>50 cm</u> from your face, ensuring that the text looks like this, not sᴉɥʇ. Alternatively, place the book on a <u>horizontal</u> surface (e.g. a table or desk) and sit adjacent to the book, at a distance which doesn't make the text too small to read.
- In case of emergency, press the two halves of the book together <u>firmly</u> in order to close.
- Before attempting to use this book, familiarise yourself with the following <u>safety information</u>:

The questions are arranged into sub-topics, so you can get exam practice on exactly the bit of your course that you want.

There are warm-up questions for the trickier sub-topics, to ease you in and get you thinking along the right lines.

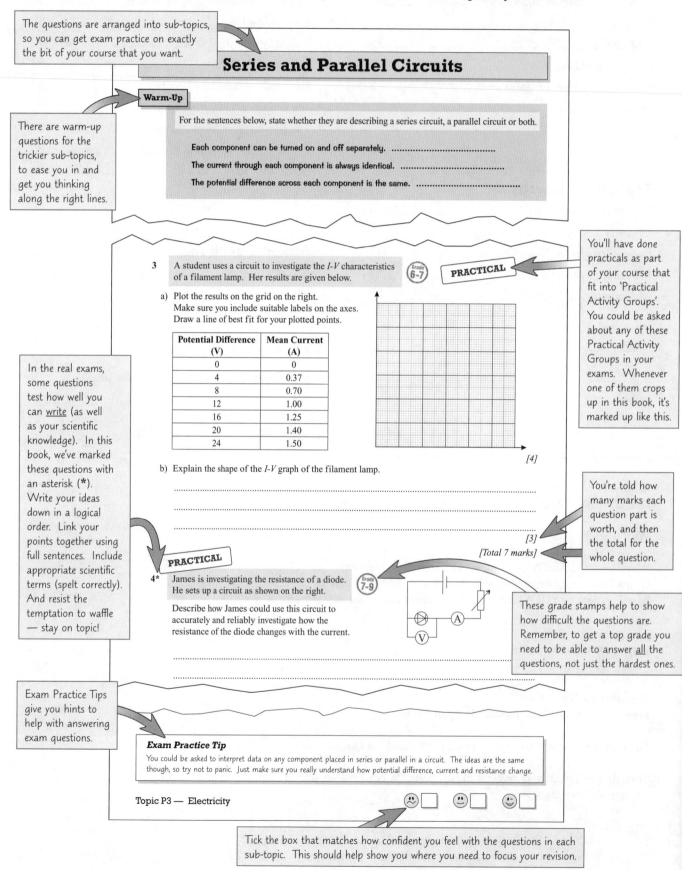

Series and Parallel Circuits

Warm-Up

For the sentences below, state whether they are describing a series circuit, a parallel circuit or both.

Each component can be turned on and off separately. ....

The current through each component is always identical. ....

The potential difference across each component is the same. ....

You'll have done practicals as part of your course that fit into 'Practical Activity Groups'. You could be asked about any of these Practical Activity Groups in your exams. Whenever one of them crops up in this book, it's marked up like this.

3   A student uses a circuit to investigate the *I-V* characteristics of a filament lamp. Her results are given below.

Grade 6-7   **PRACTICAL**

a) Plot the results on the grid on the right.
   Make sure you include suitable labels on the axes.
   Draw a line of best fit for your plotted points.

Potential Difference (V)	Mean Current (A)
0	0
4	0.37
8	0.70
12	1.00
16	1.25
20	1.40
24	1.50

[4]

b) Explain the shape of the *I-V* graph of the filament lamp.

....

....

....

[3]

[Total 7 marks]

In the real exams, some questions test how well you can <u>write</u> (as well as your scientific knowledge). In this book, we've marked these questions with an asterisk (*****). Write your ideas down in a logical order. Link your points together using full sentences. Include appropriate scientific terms (spelt correctly). And resist the temptation to waffle — stay on topic!

PRACTICAL

4* James is investigating the resistance of a diode. He sets up a circuit as shown on the right.

Grade 7-9

Describe how James could use this circuit to accurately and reliably investigate how the resistance of the diode changes with the current.

....

....

You're told how many marks each question part is worth, and then the total for the whole question.

These grade stamps help to show how difficult the questions are. Remember, to get a top grade you need to be able to answer <u>all</u> the questions, not just the hardest ones.

Exam Practice Tips give you hints to help with answering exam questions.

Exam Practice Tip
You could be asked to interpret data on any component placed in series or parallel in a circuit. The ideas are the same though, so try not to panic. Just make sure you really understand how potential difference, current and resistance change.

Topic P3 — Electricity

Tick the box that matches how confident you feel with the questions in each sub-topic. This should help show you where you need to focus your revision.

The History of the Atom and Atomic Structure

Warm-Up

Use the words below to correctly fill in the gaps in the passage.
You don't have to use every word, but each word can only be used once.

An atom is made up of .... surrounded by ....

An atom is mostly made up of .... The diameter of an atom is about

.... and the diameter of a nucleus is about ....

empty space	1×10^{15} m	neutrons	electrons
protons	1×10^{-10} m	a nucleus	1×10^{-15} m

1   A lithium nucleus contains 3 protons and 3 neutrons. Which row of the table correctly shows the relative mass and relative charge of the lithium nucleus?   **Grade 4-6**

	Mass	Charge
A	6	−3
B	3	+6
C	6	+3
D	3	−6

Your answer ☐

[Total 1 mark]

2   The theory of the structure of atoms has changed over time.   **Grade 6-7**

a) Describe the experiment carried out by Rutherford, Geiger and Marsden, and explain how it disproved Thomson's model.

....

....

....

....

....

....

[3]

b) How are electrons arranged around atoms in Bohr's model of the atom?

....

[1]

[Total 4 marks]

2

Density

1 Rachael has a mass balance, a measuring beaker and some acetic acid.

a) Describe an experiment that Rachael can carry out to calculate the density of acetic acid, using the equipment listed.

....

....

....

....

....

[4]

b) The density of acetic acid is 1.05 g/cm³. What would be the mass of 200 cm³ of acetic acid?

    A   210 g
    B   190 g
    C   0.005 kg
    D   190 kg

Your answer ▢

[1]

[Total 5 marks]

2 The titanium bar shown in the diagram has a mass of 90.0 kg.

area = 0.050 m²

length = 0.40 m

a) Calculate the density of titanium in **kg/m³**.

Density = ... kg/m³
[3]

b) What is this density in **g/cm³**?

Density = ... g/cm³
[1]

[Total 4 marks]

Topic P1 — Matter

Particle Theory and States of Matter

1 The three states of matter are solid, liquid and gas. Grade 4-6

a) Which sentence is **correct** about the density of the different states of the same substance?

  A A liquid is usually less dense than a gas.
  B A liquid is usually more dense than a solid.
  C A solid is usually more dense than a gas.
  D A solid, liquid and gas usually have the same density.

  Your answer ☐

[1]

b) What is the name of the process that occurs when a solid changes directly to a gas?

....

[1]

[Total 2 marks]

2 Joe leaves a closed plastic bottle with some water in it on a windowsill on a hot day. In the afternoon, he notices that the volume of liquid water has decreased. Grade 6-7

a) Explain in terms of the particles in the water, why the volume of liquid water in the bottle has decreased during the day.

....

....

....

....

....

[3]

b) Explain what happens to the total mass of the bottle and its contents during the day.

....

....

....

[2]

c) The next morning, Joe notices that the water is back to the same level as the previous morning. How does this show that a physical change, and **not** a chemical change, has taken place?

....

....

[2]

[Total 7 marks]

Topic P1 — Matter

Specific Heat Capacity

PRACTICAL

1* A student carries out an experiment to find the specific heat capacity of aluminium. The diagram shows her setup. Describe how the student should carry out the experiment, including how she should make the experiment more accurate.

immersion heater

aluminium cylinder

joulemeter →

thermometer

cup packed with cotton wool

....

....

....

....

....

....

....

....

[Total 6 marks]

2 A pan of water is heated on a hob. The specific heat capacity of water is 4200 J/kg°C. **Grade 6-7**

a) Define the term specific heat capacity.

....

....

[1]

b) The hob transfers 302 400 J of energy to 1.2 kg of water in the pan. If the initial temperature of the water is 24°C, calculate the temperature of the water after it has been heated. Use the formula: **change in thermal energy = mass × specific heat capacity × change in temperature.**

Temperature = ... °C

[2]

[Total 3 marks]

Exam Practice Tip

Different substances have different specific heat capacities, e.g. water has a higher specific heat capacity than alcohol. You don't need to remember any specific heat capacity values though, you'll be given them in the exam if you need them.

Topic P1 — Matter

Specific Latent Heat

The graph shows temperature against time of a substance that is being heated.
Use the words below to correctly label the graph.
You don't have to use every word, but each word can only be used once.

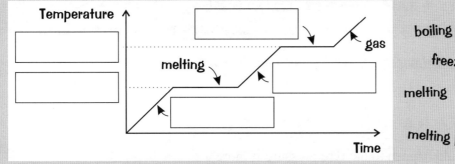

boiling point   gas

freezing   solid

melting   condensing

boiling

melting point   liquid

1 The table shows the mass and specific latent heat of vaporisation
of substances A-D. Which substance requires the **most energy** to
completely boil it (without changing its temperature)?

Substance	Mass / kg	Specific latent heat of vaporisation / J/kg
A	1	1.5
B	1	1.0
C	2	1.5
D	2	2.0

Your answer ☐

[Total 1 mark]

2 A car is parked on a street overnight. During the night, the temperature
drops low enough for 1400 g of water to condense on the car.
When the temperature is low enough, the water freezes.

a) If 462 J of energy is released from the water as it freezes,
calculate the specific latent heat of fusion of water. Use the formula:
thermal energy for a change in state = mass × specific latent heat. Show your working.

Specific latent heat of fusion = ... J/kg
[3]

b) What happens to the temperature of this water as it freezes?

....

[1]

[Total 4 marks]

Topic P1 — Matter

Pressure of Gases

Circle the correct words or phrases below so that the sentences are correct.

A gas exerts a force on a container due to <u>collisions</u> / <u>radioactivity</u>. The particles are always moving in <u>the same direction</u> / <u>random directions</u>. When the particles collide with the walls of the container, they exert <u>magnetism</u> / <u>a force</u> on it. This creates a net force <u>at right angles</u> / <u>parallel</u> to the container walls.

1 A tyre is pumped up to its maximum volume.

a) Explain what would happen to the tyre pressure if more air were pumped in, but its volume remained the same.

....

....

....

[3]

b) At its maximum volume, why would the tyre pressure be higher on a hot day compared to a cold day?

....

....

....

....

[3]

[Total 6 marks]

2 Each container has the same mass of gas inside. In which container is the pressure the **highest**?

A Volume = 0.04 m³
Temperature = 10°C

B  Volume = 0.04 m³
Temperature = 20°C

C  Volume = 40 000 cm³
Temperature = 10°C

D Volume = 40 000 cm³
Temperature = 30°C

Your answer ☐

[Total 1 mark]

3   A test tube has a deflated balloon covering
its open end, so that no air can get in or out.
The test tube is put in a beaker of cold water.

Grade 6-7

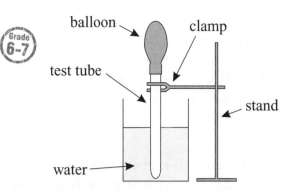

a) The water is heated to 80°C. As the water gets hotter, the balloon starts to inflate. Explain why.

....

....

....

....

....

....

....

[5]

b) The water is kept at a constant temperature of 80°C
so that the balloon stays at a constant volume.
The diagram shows force arrows which represent
the net forces acting inside and outside part of the
balloon's surface. Circle the **two** arrows that are
incorrect and explain why they are incorrect.

inside ⇨ ⇦ outside

part of the
surface of the balloon

....

....

....

[4]

c) The procedure is repeated with an identical test tube sealed with a rubber bung, so that the initial
volume of trapped air is the same in both experiments. Compare the pressure in the tube with the
bung to the pressure in the tube with the balloon as the water is heated. Explain your reasoning.

....

....

....

....

....

[4]

[Total 13 marks]

Topic P1 — Matter

4   The diagram shows a large
    syringe filled with helium gas
    and sealed with a plunger, at
    a pressure of 1.1×10^5 Pa and
    temperature 24°C.

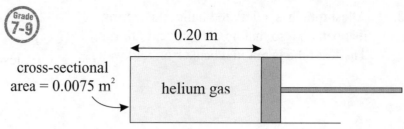

cross-sectional
area = 0.0075 m²

0.20 m

helium gas

a) i) The helium is kept at a constant temperature and the plunger is pulled out.
        Explain the change in pressure which occurs.

        ....

        ....

        [2]

   ii) The volume of the helium gas is now 2.75×10^{-3} m³ and its temperature is still 24°C.
        Use the formula **pressure × volume = constant** to calculate the pressure of the helium now.

        A 3×10^5 Pa
        B 1.5×10^{-3} Pa
        C 6×10^4 Pa
        D 6×10^{-4} Pa

        Your answer ☐

        [1]

b) The plunger is then released and moves until it reaches an equilibrium position and stops moving.
    Explain why.

    ....

    ....

    ....

    ....

    ....

    [3]

c) The plunger is then pushed in again, compressing the helium.
    Suggest why the temperature of the helium might change.

    ....

    ....

    ....

    ....

    ....

    [4]

    [Total 10 marks]

Exam Practice Tip

Just make sure you know how to work with standard form on your calculator, and practise doing so. And remember,
it's not scary, it's just a short-hand way of writing long numbers. For example, $1.1 \times 10^5 = 110\ 000$.

Topic P1 — Matter

 ☐   ☐   ☺ ☐

Atmospheric Pressure and Liquid Pressure

For each of the following statements, circle whether the statement is **true** or **false**.

The Earth's atmosphere reaches the Sun.	True /	False
Atmospheric pressure acts in all directions.	True /	False
The higher up you go, the more atmosphere there is above you.	True /	False

1 The pressure of the atmosphere varies with height.

a) A helicopter flies vertically upwards.
What happens to the atmospheric pressure and density around the helicopter as it moves up?

	Pressure	Density
A	Increases	Increases
B	Increases	Decreases
C	Decreases	Increases
D	Decreases	Decreases

Your answer ☐

[1]

b) Why does atmospheric pressure vary with height?

....

....

[2]

[Total 3 marks]

2 Liquid pressure can vary with depth.

a) Which sentence is correct about the **density** of sea water?
A Density at 10 m below surface = density at 50 m below surface.
B Density at 10 m below surface > density at 50 m below surface.
C Density at 10 m below surface < density at 50 m below surface.
D Density at 10 m below surface $\propto$ density at 50 m below surface.

Your answer ☐

[1]

b) A submarine is stationary at 100 m below the surface of the water. It then dives down to 200 m.
Use the formula: **pressure due to a column of liquid = height of column × density of liquid × g**
to explain what will happen to the pressure exerted on the submarine by the water.

....

....

....

[3]

[Total 4 marks]

3   Scientists are measuring the pressure at different depths in a new liquid.
     The table shows the results from the experiment.

Depth (m)	Pressure measured (Pa)				Mean pressure (Pa)
	Test 1	Test 2	Test 3	Test 4	
10	1.10×10^5	1.15×10^5	1.08×10^5	1.15×10^5	1.12×10^5
20	2.44×10^5	2.40×10^5	2.42×10^5	3.69×10^5	
30	3.40×10^5	3.41×10^5	3.41×10^5	3.40×10^5	3.40×10^5
40	4.63×10^5	4.63×10^5	4.62×10^5	4.64×10^5	4.63×10^5

a) i) Complete the table above by calculating the mean pressure at 20 m.

[2]

ii) Why is it important to calculate a mean?

....

[1]

b) i) Use the data collected from a depth of 30 m and 40 m to calculate the density of the liquid.
        Use: **pressure due to a column of liquid = height of column × density of liquid × _g_**
        and gravitational field strength (_g_) = 10 N/kg. Show your working.

Density = ... kg/m³

[4]

ii) Suggest why the data from 30 m and 40 m is the most sensible to use for this calculation.

....

....

....

[2]

c) An object with a density of 655 kg/m³ is placed on the liquid.
    Explain what would happen to the object.

....

....

....

[3]

[Total 12 marks]

Exam Practice Tip

Always show your working, whether you're asked to or not, and include any equations you've used and how you've
rearranged them. It'll help you check your working and you could still get some marks even if your final answer is wrong.

Topic P1 — Matter

Speed and Velocity

Put the following quantities under the correct heading to show if they're scalar or vector quantities.

acceleration   speed

distance

velocity

displacement

Scalar	Vector

1   Nick is walking at a constant speed of 1.5 m/s.

a) How far has he walked in 120 s? Give the unit.

Distance = ... Unit ....

[3]

b) Nick then starts jogging. He jogs 5100 m in 34 minutes. What is Nick's average jogging speed?

Speed = ... m/s

[3]

[Total 6 marks]

2   Suma is driving **east** at 50 km/hr.

a) What is Suma's speed in m/s?

A   180 m/s
B   13.9 m/s
C   18 m/s
D   1.39 m/s

Your answer ☐

[1]

b) The road turns so Suma is now driving **north** at 50 km/hr.
    Explain why her velocity has changed but her speed hasn't.

....

....

....

[2]

[Total 3 marks]

Acceleration

1 Trigger the dog sets off running from rest and reaches a speed of 3.2 m/s in 8.0 s.

a) Find Trigger's acceleration. Give the unit.

Acceleration = ... Unit ....

[3]

b) She keeps running with this acceleration for a further 6.0 s. Calculate Trigger's final speed. Show your working.

Speed = ... m/s

[3]

c) Trigger continues to run at this final speed in circular loops around the garden. Which statement is **correct**?

A   Trigger is accelerating, but her velocity is constant.
B   Trigger is accelerating and her velocity is changing.
C   Trigger is not accelerating, but her velocity is constant.
D   Trigger is not accelerating and her velocity is changing.

Your answer ☐

[1]

[Total 7 marks]

2 A boat is travelling at a constant velocity of 5.0 m/s. It then starts to accelerate with a constant acceleration of 0.25 m/s² for a distance of 1.2×10^3 m.

a) Find the final velocity of the boat. Use the formula:
(final velocity)² – (initial velocity)² = 2 × acceleration × distance.

Velocity = ... m/s

[2]

b) Calculate the time it takes for the boat to travel this distance.

Time = ... s

[3]

[Total 5 marks]

Exam Practice Tip

Remember that displacement, velocity and acceleration are all vector quantities, which means they have both a magnitude and a direction. Whereas distance and speed are scalar quantities, and so they only have a magnitude (no direction).

Investigating Motion

1 Alice wants to carry out an experiment to investigate the motion of a trolley down a ramp. Her textbook suggests setting up her apparatus as shown in the diagram.

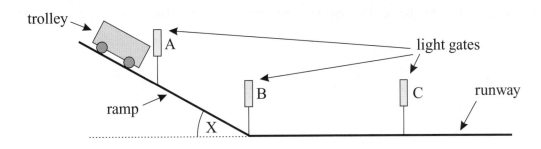

a)* Describe how Alice could use this apparatus to find the **acceleration** of the trolley down the ramp.

....

....

....

....

....

....

....

[6]

b) Alice wants to calculate the average speed of the trolley on the runway. But she can't find any light gates, so she decides to use a stopwatch instead.

i) What measurements would Alice need to make to determine the average speed of the trolley on the **runway** now? Explain your answer.

....

....

....

[3]

ii) Give **one** disadvantage of using a stopwatch instead of light gates.

....

[1]

c) What would happen to the speed of the trolley on the runway if the angle labelled X in the diagram was **increased**?

....

[1]

[Total 11 marks]

Topic P2 — Forces

Distance-Time Graphs

1 Simon walks to work. He starts off at a steady speed, before stopping for a quick drink of water. He then travels at a steady speed again, but faster than before.

Sketch a line on the axes below to show the distance-time graph for Simon's walk to work.

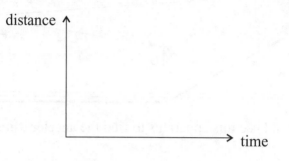

[Total 3 marks]

2 The graph shows the distance-time graph for a car journey.

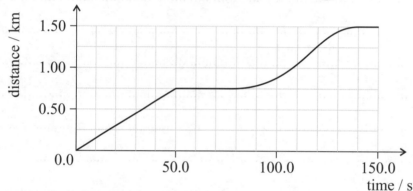

a) Describe the car journey using data from the graph.

....

....

....

....

....

[4]

b) i) Calculate the car's average speed between 80.0 s and 140.0 s.
Give your answer in m/s.

Speed = ... m/s
[3]

ii) Calculate the car's speed at 100.0 s.

Speed = ... m/s
[3]

[Total 10 marks]

Topic P2 — Forces

Velocity-Time Graphs

Use two of the phrases from the list below to correctly label the velocity-time graph.

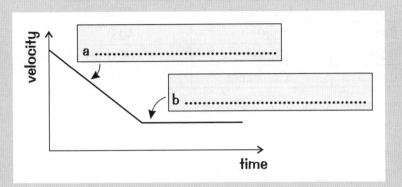

decreasing deceleration

steady speed

decreasing acceleration

constant acceleration

constant deceleration

1   Velocity-time graphs can be used to show the motion of an object.

Which quantity is represented by the area under a velocity-time graph?

A   speed
B   acceleration
C   distance
D   deceleration

Your answer ☐

[Total 1 mark]

2   A bear runs with a constant acceleration for 10 s before running at a constant velocity
of 8 m/s for a further 10 s. Which of the following velocity-time graphs shows this?

A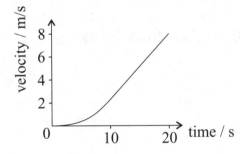

B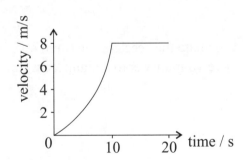

C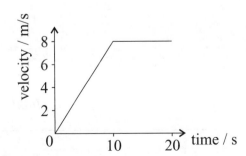

D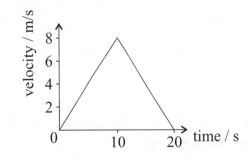

Your answer ☐

[Total 1 mark]

3   A lorry is driving along a straight road. The table shows the acceleration of the lorry during different time periods and the lorry's velocity at the end of each time period.

Time period (hours)	Acceleration	Final velocity (mph)
0.00 - 0.10	Constant	20.0
0.10 - 0.20	Increasing	24.0
0.20 - 0.30	Increasing	40.0
0.30 - 0.40	0	40.0
0.40 - 0.50	Constant	60.0
0.50 - 0.60	Constant	0.0

a) Complete the velocity-time graph for the lorry's journey.
    The first 0.30 hours have been done for you.

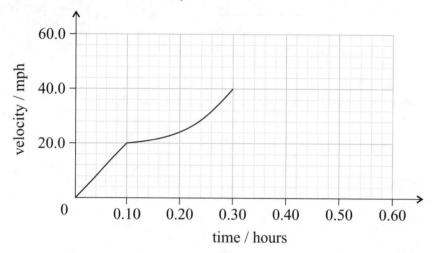

[3]

b) How far does the lorry travel in the first 0.30 hours?

Distance = ... miles

[3]

c) Calculate the acceleration (in m/s^2) of the lorry at 0.20 hours. 1 mile = 1600 m.
    Give your answer to **2** significant figures.

Acceleration = ... m/s^2

[5]

[Total 11 marks]

Exam Practice Tip

A velocity-time graph doesn't just tell you what the velocity of an object is, it can also be used to find the distance travelled by the object and its acceleration throughout its journey. That's a lot of information on one graph.

Forces and Free Body Force Diagrams

1 The diagram shows a free body force diagram for a truck.

a) What is the magnitude and direction of the resultant force?

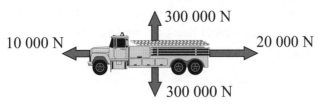

A 10 000 N to the left
B 20 000 N to the left
C 30 000 N to the right
D 10 000 N to the right

Your answer ☐

[1]

b) What do we mean by the resultant force acting on an object?

....

....

[2]

[Total 3 marks]

2 A toy car is at rest on a table. A free body force diagram of the car is shown.

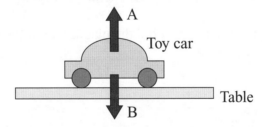

a) Name the forces that are labelled A and B in the diagram.

A = ...   B = ...

[2]

b) Describe the resultant force acting on the car.

....

[1]

c) Someone pushes the car, so it starts to move towards the left.

   i) Draw and label arrows on the diagram to show the new forces acting on the car.

[3]

   ii) Describe the resultant force acting on the toy car now.

....

[1]

[Total 7 marks]

Scale Diagrams and Forces

1   Which of the following sentences is **correct** for an object that is in equilibrium?

    A   All the forces acting on the object cancel each other out.

    B   All the forces acting on the object must act in the same direction.

    C   All the forces acting on the object must be the same size.

    D   There is only one force acting on the object.

Your answer ☐

[Total 1 mark]

2   Which of the following shows the correct way to resolve a force (solid line) into it's horizontal and vertical component forces (dotted lines).

    A   **B**   **C**   **D**

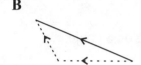 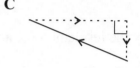 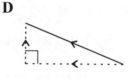

Your answer ☐

[Total 1 mark]

3   A light aircraft is flying north-east in a straight line. The aircraft's engine provides a force of 600 N north. A strong wind is blowing in an easterly direction and provides a force of 800 N on the aircraft.

Draw a scale drawing on the grid below. Find the magnitude of the resultant force on the aircraft.

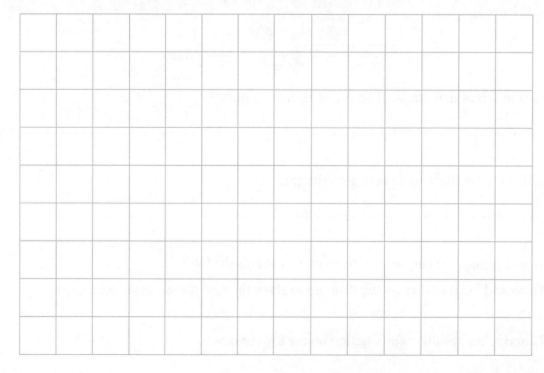

Resultant force = ... N

[Total 3 marks]

Topic P2 — Forces

4 A toy dog on wheels can be pulled along with a piece of string. The string is at an angle to the ground, but the toy dog moves forwards along the ground at a steady speed. A scale diagram of this is shown below.

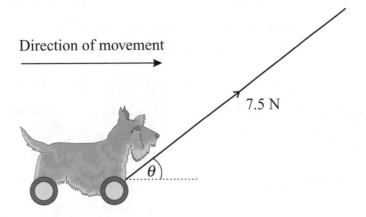

Direction of movement

7.5 N

θ

a) i) Using the diagram, find the force acting on the toy dog in the direction of its movement.

Force = ... N

[3]

  ii) What is the magnitude of the frictional force acting on the dog?

  A   4.5 N
  B   6 N
  C   1.5 N
  D   7.5 N

  Your answer ☐

[1]

b) The normal contact force acting on the toy dog from the ground is 1.5 N.
Find the weight of the toy dog.

Weight = ... N

[3]

The toy dog is now pulled along so that the angle, θ, increases but the magnitude of the force stays the same.

c) Explain what will happen to the speed of the dog.

....

....

....

[3]

[Total 10 marks]

Topic P2 — Forces

Newton's First and Second Laws of Motion

Use the words below to correctly fill in the gaps in the passage.
You don't have to use every word, but each word can only be used once.

Newton's First Law of motion says that an object will remain stationary or moving at

.... if there is .... resultant force acting on it.

If there is .... resultant force acting, it will ....

a constant velocity	accelerate	a zero
a non-zero	remain stationary	an increasing speed

1   A rocket is moving at a constant velocity in space (a vacuum).
    In order to change its velocity, it turns on its thrusters, accelerates
    to the desired velocity and then turns them off again.

    Grade 4-6

a) The mass of the rocket is 110 000 kg and it accelerates at 5.0 m/s^2.
    What force is provided by the thrusters?

    A   550 000 N
    B   55 000 N
    C   22 000 N
    D   220 000 N

    Your answer ☐

    [1]

b) After the rocket has turned off its thrusters, the rocket continues moving at a constant velocity.
    Use Newton's First Law to explain why.

    ....

    ....

    ....
    [2]
    [Total 3 marks]

2   A sailboat has a mass of 60 kg and is accelerating at 0.4 m/s^2. The wind acting on the
    sail provides a force of 44 N. The drag from the water acts in the opposite direction.

    Grade 6-7

    Calculate the force of the drag acting on the boat. Show your working.

    Force = ... N
    [Total 3 marks]

3 Meena has been using the apparatus below to investigate the effect of force on the acceleration of a trolley. The trolley is on a frictionless, flat surface.

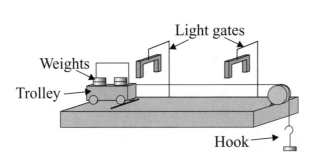 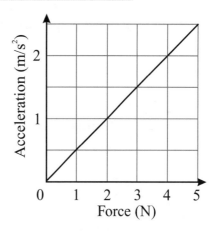

When the hook is allowed to fall, the trolley accelerates. Meena records the force acting on the trolley and calculates its acceleration. Meena repeats this process, each time moving a 1 N weight from the trolley to the hook. She draws a graph of mean acceleration against force for the trolley.

a) Which **two** measurements must Meena record in order to calculate the acceleration of the trolley?

....

....

[2]

b) Give **one** conclusion you can draw from Meena's graph.

....

[1]

c) Calculate the mass of the system.

Mass = ... kg

[3]

[Total 6 marks]

4 A car of mass 1.5×10^3 kg accelerates uniformly from rest. It reaches 23 m/s in 7.0 s.

Calculate the force needed to cause this acceleration.
Give your answer to **2** significant figures.

Force = ... N

[Total 4 marks]

Topic P2 — Forces

Friction and Terminal Velocity

1 Which of the following graphs shows an object that is reaching terminal velocity?

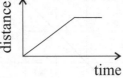

A

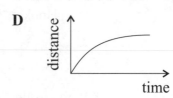

B

C

D

Your answer ☐

[Total 1 mark]

2 Which statement describes the forces acting when an object is travelling at terminal velocity?

A   driving force > friction force
B   driving force < friction force
C   driving force = friction force
D   driving force ∝ friction force

Your answer ☐

[Total 1 mark]

3* A student drops a large book and a cricket ball that both have the same weight from a tall building. Explain why both objects eventually reach terminal velocity. Compare the magnitude of each object's terminal velocity.

....

....

....

....

....

....

....

[Total 6 marks]

Exam Practice Tip

Remember that the acceleration of a falling object on Earth is always changing because of the air resistance acting on it. That means you won't be able to use any of those equations for uniform acceleration (unless you ignore air resistance).

Topic P2 — Forces

Inertia and Newton's Third Law of Motion

1   The inertia of an object is dependent on its mass.   *Grade 4-6*

a)   What do we mean by the term inertia?

....

[1]

b)   A ball is rolling freely along a table. There is a frictional force of 0.50 mN acting on the ball, so that it's decelerating at 0.0025 m/s². Calculate the mass of the ball.

Mass = ... kg

[3]

[Total 4 marks]

2   Dave is at rest on his skateboard (combined mass of 80 kg). He pushes a wall with a force of 24 N. You can assume there is no friction between the skateboard and the ground.   *Grade 6-7*

a)   Explain why Dave would move away from the wall.

....

....

....

[2]

b)   Dave's brother goes on the skateboard and pushes away from the wall with the same force. His mass combined with the skateboard is 40 kg. What is the difference in their accelerations?

A   0.3 m/s²
B   0.6 m/s²
C   1.6 m/s²
D   3.3 m/s²

Your answer ☐

[1]

[Total 3 marks]

3   A plate in equilibrium is sat on a table. Explain why $W_E = R_T$.   *Grade 7-9*

R_P = normal contact force of table pushing up on plate
R_T = normal contact force of plate pushing down on table
W_P = gravitational force of Earth pulling down on plate
W_E = gravitational force of plate pulling up on Earth

....

....

....

....

[Total 4 marks]

Topic P2 — Forces

Momentum and Conservation of Momentum

Warm-Up

Circle the correct words or phrases below so that the sentences are correct.

In a collision where <u>no other</u> / <u>two other</u> external forces act,

momentum is <u>increased</u> / <u>conserved</u>.

This means that the momentum before <u>equals</u> / <u>is double</u> the momentum after.

When a <u>zero</u> / <u>non-zero</u> resultant force acts on an object for a certain

amount of time, it causes a change in momentum.

1   A vehicle is moving east with a velocity of 15 m/s and momentum 46 000 kg m/s.

a) Calculate the mass of the vehicle.
   Give your answer to **2** significant figures.

Mass = ... kg

[3]

b) A vehicle of half the mass is driving west at the same speed.
   What is the momentum of this vehicle?

   A   −46 000 kg m/s
   B   46 000 kg m/s
   C   −23 000 kg m/s
   D   23 000 kg m/s

   Your answer ☐

[1]

[Total 4 marks]

2   A full trailer is pulled by a car travelling north at 20 mph. The car
    stops and the trailer is unloaded, which halves the mass of the trailer.
    The car travels back south at 40 mph.

How will the trailer's momentum have changed compared to when it was travelling north?

	Momentum magnitude	Momentum sign
A	Doubles	Changes from positive to negative
B	No change	Changes from positive to negative
C	Doubles	No change
D	Halves	No change

Your answer ☐

[Total 1 mark]

3 A stationary red ball is hit by a blue ball with mass 4.5×10^{-1} kg and velocity 3.0 m/s. The balls collide elastically then move off together at 2.5 m/s.

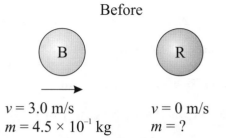

Before

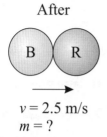

After

$v = 3.0$ m/s
$m = 4.5 \times 10^{-1}$ kg

$v = 0$ m/s
$m = ?$

$v = 2.5$ m/s
$m = ?$

a) Calculate the mass of the red ball.

Mass = ... kg

[3]

b) What is meant by an elastic collision?

....

....

[1]

[Total 4 marks]

4 Ball A has a mass of 2.0 kg. Ball B has a mass of 3.0 kg. Both are moving in the same direction. Ball A is moving faster than ball B, so the two collide. After the collision, both balls move off together in the same direction.

Just before the collision, ball A has a velocity of 1.7 m/s and ball B has a velocity of 1.2 m/s.
3.0 s after the collision, the two balls have a velocity of 0.50 m/s.
Calculate the magnitude of the frictional force acting on the two balls after the collision.
Show your working.

Force = ... N

[Total 5 marks]

Topic P2 — Forces

Mass, Weight and Gravity

Warm-Up

State whether each of the following statements are true or false.

1) The gravitational field strength on Earth is 10 N/kg. ....

2) The larger an object, the smaller its gravitational field strength. ....

3) The weight of an object is the same everywhere in the universe. ....

4) The mass of an object is the same everywhere in the universe. ....

1 Mia weighs 650 N on Earth.

  a) Define the term weight.

....
                                            [1]

  b) Calculate Mia's mass on Earth. Use: gravitational field strength (g) = 10 N/kg.

Mass = ... kg
[2]
[Total 3 marks]

2 An astronaut on the Moon drops her screwdriver.

Use data from the table to calculate the acceleration of the screwdriver as it falls towards the Moon. Use: g = 10 N/kg. Give your answer to **2** significant figures.

	On Earth	On the Moon
Weight (N)	4.6×10^{-1}	7.5×10^{-2}

Acceleration = ... m/s²
[Total 4 marks]

Exam Practice Tip

Outside of physics, people often use the term weight when they mean mass. Make sure you get the differences straight in your head. You measure mass on a set of scales, but weight is a force measured by a spring-balance (newtonmeter).

Mechanical Energy Stores

1 Sarah has a mass of 65 kg and climbs up some stairs from the ground floor of a building to a height of 10 m.

Calculate the amount of energy in Sarah's gravitational potential energy store at the top of the stairs.

Energy = ... J

[Total 3 marks]

2 Cars A-D are all travelling at a constant speed.

a) The masses and speeds of the cars are shown in the table.
Which car has the **most** energy in its kinetic energy store?

	Mass (kg)	Speed (m/s)
A	1500	11
B	1000	15
C	1800	10
D	2000	8

Your answer ☐

[1]

Car A is parked at the top of a hill. The driver releases the handbrake and allows the car to roll freely down the hill. When the car reaches the bottom of the hill, it is travelling at 43.2 km/hr. If you ignore friction and air resistance, the energy in the kinetic energy store of the car at the bottom of the hill equals the energy in the gravitational potential energy store of the car at the top of the hill.

b) Calculate the height of the hill. Use: gravitational field strength (g) = 10 N/kg.

Height = ... m

[4]

[Total 5 marks]

Topic P2 — Forces

Work Done and Power

1 All bulbs have a power rating. *(Grade 4-6)*

a) Which statement is **correct** for a 60 W bulb?

   A   It transfers 60 J of energy every second.
   B   It transfers 60 J of energy every 2 seconds.
   C   It transfers 60 J of energy every hour.
   D   It transfers 60 kJ of energy every second.

Your answer [ ]

[1]

b) How much energy will a 40 W bulb transfer in 1 minute?

   A   40 J
   B   40 kJ
   C   2400 J
   D   2400 W

Your answer [ ]

[1]

[Total 2 marks]

2 A box is pulled along a frozen pond by an electric winch with a 21.0 N force. It takes 12.5 s for the box to be dragged 35.0 m to the edge of the pond. You can assume the friction between the box and the ice is negligible. *(Grade 6-7)*

a) i) Calculate the work done on the box.

Work done = ... Unit ....
[3]

ii) Calculate the power of the winch.

Power = ... W
[2]

b) The force pulling the box is removed at the edge of the pond. The box then slides onto a paved path, where it slows down to a stop. The frictional force acting on the box from the path is 17.5 N. Calculate the distance the box travels before stopping.

Distance = ... m
[3]

[Total 8 marks]

Topic P2 — Forces

3 Siobhan needs a motor with a power of 0.6 W for her experiment. She finds four unlabelled motors in her lab. She sets up the experiment shown on the right and times how long it takes each motor to lift a 5000 g mass over the distance labelled X in the diagram.

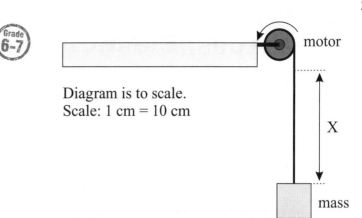

Diagram is to scale.
Scale: 1 cm = 10 cm

Her results are shown in the table below. Which motor should Siobhan use?
Use the formula: **potential energy = mass × height × gravitational field strength (10 N/kg)**

Motor	Time (s)
A	0.4
B	16
C	25
D	40

Your answer ☐

[Total 1 mark]

4 A car manufacturer is testing the brakes on a new brand of sports car. At top speed, the brakes bring the car to a stop in 365 m. The brakes work with a force of 8.1×10^3 N and the mass of the car is 1225 kg.

Calculate the top speed of the car.
Show your working.

Speed = ... m/s
[Total 4 marks]

Exam Practice Tip

When work is done on a object, energy is transferred to an energy store of the object, e.g. the kinetic energy store of an object being pushed. So you might have to use multiple equations in one question, e.g. work done and kinetic energy.

 ☐   ☐   ☐

Forces, Elasticity and Hooke's Law

1 Claire wants to stretch a spring of resting length 72 mm and spring constant 24 N/m.

a) What is the minimum number of forces Claire must apply to the spring in order to stretch it?

....
[1]

Claire clamps the spring at one end and pulls the other end. It stretches to 87 mm.

b) i) Calculate the force that Claire is applying to the spring.

Force = ... N
[3]

ii) Calculate the energy transferred to the spring during this stretching.
Use the formula: **energy transferred in stretching = 0.5 × spring constant × (extension)²**
Give the unit.

Energy = ... Unit ....
[2]

c) The spring displays elastic deformation. What does this mean?

....
[1]

[Total 7 marks]

2 Spring A has a smaller spring constant than spring B. They both reach their elastic limit when they have been extended by the same amount.

Which of the following correctly shows the force-extension graphs for both springs?
The elastic limits are marked with a dot.

A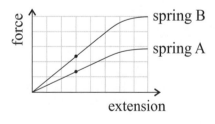

B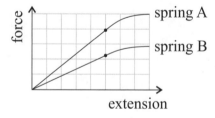

C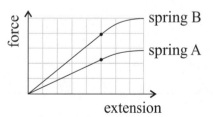

D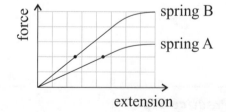

Your answer ☐

[Total 1 mark]

PRACTICAL

3 Michael is investigating the effect of force on the extension of two different springs, X and Y. For each spring, he clamps the top of the spring and hangs different numbers of 1 N weights from the bottom of the spring, then measures the extension with a ruler. A table of Michael's results and a graph of spring X is shown below.

Spring X

Force (N)	Extension (cm)	
	X	Y
0	0	0
1	3.0	4.0
2	6.0	8.0
3	9.0	12.0
4	12.5	16.9
5	17.5	30.0
6	29.0	—

a) i) The force-extension graph for spring X is shown above.
Draw the force-extension graph for spring Y on the same axes.

[3]

ii) Describe and explain the shape of the graph you have drawn.

....

....

....

....

....

[4]

b) Using the graph you have drawn, calculate the spring constant of **spring Y**.

Spring constant = ... N/m

[3]

c) Use the graph to find the energy transferred to **spring X** as it was extended by 12.5 cm to 17.5 cm, assuming it has not passed its elastic limit.

Energy transferred = ... J

[2]

d) Suggest **one** safety precaution that Michael should take when carrying out the investigation.

....

[1]

[Total 13 marks]

Topic P2 — Forces

Moments

1 The diagram shows a box spanner used by a mechanic. He applies a force of 50 N at the end of the spanner.

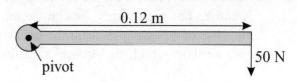

a) Calculate the size of the moment created. Give the unit.

Moment = ... Unit.......................

[3]

b) In which direction will the spanner turn?

....

[1]

[Total 4 marks]

2 Two people reach a manual revolving door at the same time. Each person pushes one wing of the door with a different force and at a different distance from the pivot, as shown in the diagram below.

Diagram not to scale.

Person A pushes with force of 40 N, 0.5 m from the pivot.
Person B pushes with force of 24 N, 0.7 m from the pivot.

Would the door turn clockwise, anticlockwise or stay as it is (in equilibrium)?
Show your working.

....

[Total 3 marks]

3 The diagram shows three children on a balanced seesaw. Calculate child C's distance from the pivot. Give you answer in metres.

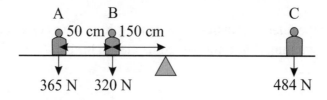

Diagram not to scale.

Distance = ... m
[Total 3 marks]

Levers and Gears

State whether each of the following statements are true or false.

Cogs can only turn clockwise. ....

A force multiplier creates a large output force for a small input force. ....

1 The diagram shows several cogs that are linked together.
If cog A is turned clockwise, in which direction will cogs B and C turn?

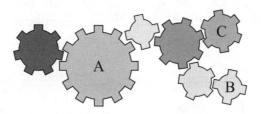

Cog B: ....   Cog C: ....

[Total 2 marks]

2 Two children are playing outside. One child, with a weight of 420 N, stands on one end of a plank of wood as shown in the diagram. The other child pushes down on the opposite end of the plank of wood.

P

Diagram not to scale.

2.4 m

0.60 m

What force should the child apply to point P in order to lift the child stood on the plank?

Force = ... N

[Total 3 marks]

3 The diagram on the right shows three cogs linked together.
Cog D completes 1.5 rotations every second.

How many rotations will cog F complete in 12 s?

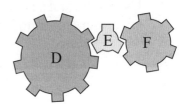

Number of rotations = ...

[Total 3 marks]

Hydraulics

1 Which of the following statements is **true?**

    A   There is only pressure in a fluid when a force is applied.
    B   Pressure in a fluid will be higher where it is closer to the force applied to the fluid.
    C   The larger the force applied to a fluid, the lower the pressure of the fluid.
    D   Pressure in fluids causes a net force at right-angles to all surfaces.

Your answer ☐

[Total 1 mark]

2 Kate is planning on building a car. She designs the hydraulic braking system to be like the one shown in the diagram below. She plans to make the brakes apply an equal braking force to all four wheels of the car.

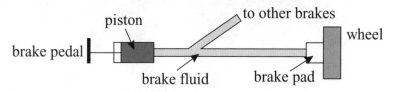

a) Kate designs the head of the piston as a square, of side length 2.50 cm. Calculate the pressure that will be transmitted throughout the hydraulic fluid if the brake is applied with a force of 115 N.

Pressure = ... Pa
[3]

b) The brake pad that will be attached to one wheel has a surface area of 0.00500 m². Calculate the total braking force that will be acting on the car.

Force = ... N
[3]
[Total 6 marks]

3 A water balloon is squeezed so that a force of 1.5 N is applied to its surface, increasing the pressure of the water by 3.2 Pa. Assuming the balloon is always spherical, find its radius when it's squeezed.

Use the formula: **surface area of a sphere = 4 × π × (radius)².**
Give your answer to **2** significant figures.

Pressure = ... Pa
[Total 3 marks]

> **Exam Practice Tip**
> That was a long topic, with lots of equations, some of which can be used together to answer questions. Make sure you know how the equations can be applied to different situations, so you'll be ready for anything the examiners throw at you.

Static Electricity

1   Static electricity is the build up of charge on an object.   Grade 4-6

  a) Which of the following statements is **true**?
     A   When two conductors are rubbed together, protons pass from one to the other.
     B   When two insulators are rubbed together, electrons pass from one to the other.
     C   When an object loses electrons, it becomes negatively charged.
     D   When an object gains electrons, it becomes positively charged.

     Your answer ☐
                                                                                        [1]

  b) All matter contains charge, but some matter is electrically neutral.
     Explain why.

     ....

     ....
                                                                                        [2]
                                                                              [Total 3 marks]

2   Kavita rubs a plastic acetate rod with a cloth. A positive static charge builds up on the rod.   Grade 6-7

  a) Explain how a static charge has built up on the rod.

     ....

     ....

     ....
                                                                                        [2]

  b) i) Kavita holds the rod close to some small scraps of paper. The scraps 'jump' towards the rod.
        Why does this happen?

     ....

     ....

     ....

     ....

     ....
                                                                                        [3]

     ii) Kavita then tries the same experiment with a metal rod, but the paper doesn't jump.
         Suggest why the experiment doesn't work with a metal rod.

     ....

     ....

     ....
                                                                                        [3]
                                                                              [Total 8 marks]

Electric Fields

1 Complete the statement. Electric field lines... *(Grade 4-6)*

     A ... always point away from a negative charge.
     B ... must always be straight.
     C ... always point towards a positive charge.
     D ... always meet a charge at right angles to its surface.

Your answer ☐

[Total 1 mark]

2 Which of the following statements is **not** correct? *(Grade 4-6)*

     A All electric charges create an electric field.
     B A charged object placed in an electric field will experience a force.
     C Charges only have an electric field when they're near other charges.
     D The closer together field lines are, the stronger the electric field.

Your answer ☐

[Total 1 mark]

3 The field lines around charges change when the charges are put near each other. *(Grade 6-7)*

a) i) Two charged spheres are placed near each other. The diagram below shows their field lines. Add labels to the diagram to show the type of charge (positive or negative) on each sphere.

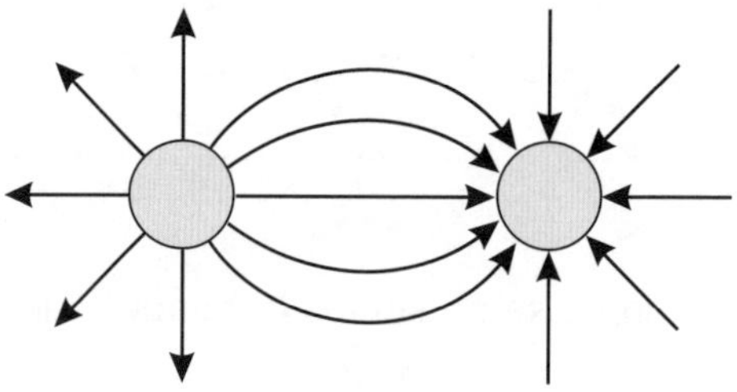

[1]

ii) Explain what would happen to the field lines if the charges were free to move.

....

....

[2]

b) A positive and negative sphere are placed near each other, as shown in the diagram below. Add field lines to the diagram to show how the two charges interact.

     ⊕   ⊕

[2]

[Total 5 marks]

Exam Practice Tip

Make sure to add arrows to any field lines that you draw — they tell you which direction the electric field is acting in.

Topic P3 — Electricity   ☹ ☐   ☺ ☐   ☺ ☐

Current and Potential Difference

Warm-Up

Use the words below to correctly fill in the gaps in the passage.
You don't have to use every word, but each word can only be used once.

.... is the rate of flow of electric charge (electrons) around a circuit.

The driving force that pushes current around a circuit is called the ....

It is the .... transferred per unit charge. A current will flow around a circuit

if the circuit is .... and there is a source of ....

energy   current

potential difference   closed   potential difference

1 A simple circuit is shown on the right.

a) How much charge passes through
the light bulb in 120 seconds?

   A 420 V

   B 34 V

   C 420 C

   D 34 C

3.5 A

Your answer ☐ *[1]*

b) Calculate how long it will take for 770 C to pass through the light bulb. Show your working.

Time = ... s

[3]

[Total 4 marks]

2 It takes 2.5 mins and 276 kJ of energy for a kettle to boil water using a supply at 230 V.

a) Calculate the amount of charge that passes through the kettle.
Use the formula: **energy transferred = charge × potential difference**

Charge = ... C

[3]

b) Calculate the current that is flowing through the circuit. Give the unit.

Current = ... unit ....

[3]

[Total 6 marks]

Topic P3 — Electricity

Circuits and Resistance

Warm-Up

Draw lines from each symbol to the name of the component that they represent.

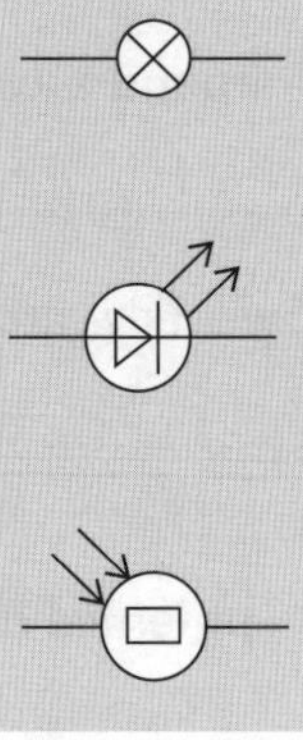

Voltmeter
Thermistor
Filament lamp
LDR
Switch
LED

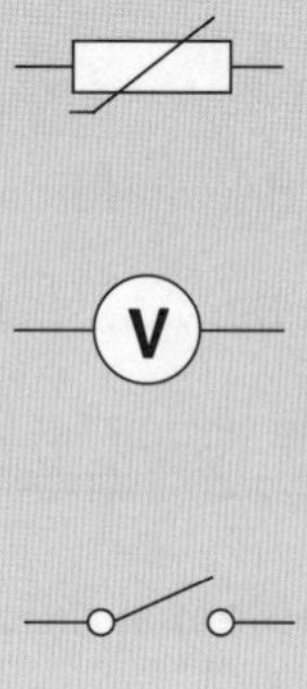

1 A current of 350 mA flows through a 5 Ω resistor. Calculate the potential difference across the resistor. Grade 4-6

Potential difference = ... V
[Total 3 marks]

2 A circuit contains a cell and a variable resistor in series and an ammeter, which is used to measure the current. Grade 6-7

a) Draw a diagram to show this circuit.

[3]

b) A current of 2.4 A flows when the resistor has a resistance of 2.5 Ω.

What should the variable resistor be set to for a current of 4.0 A to flow?

A 6 Ω
B 0.7 Ω
C 24 Ω
D 1.5 Ω

Your answer ☐

[1]
[Total 4 marks]

PRACTICAL

3 A student uses a circuit to investigate the *I-V* characteristics of a filament lamp. Her results are given below.

Grade 6-7

a) Plot the results on the grid on the right.
Make sure you include suitable labels on the axes.
Draw a line of best fit for your plotted points.

Potential Difference (V)	Mean Current (A)
0	0
4	0.37
8	0.70
12	1.00
16	1.25
20	1.40
24	1.50

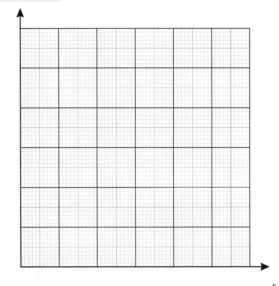

[4]

b) Explain the shape of the *I-V* graph of the filament lamp.

....

....

....

[3]

[Total 7 marks]

PRACTICAL

4* James is investigating the resistance of a diode. He sets up a circuit as shown on the right.

Grade 7-9

Describe how James could use this circuit to accurately and reliably investigate how the resistance of the diode changes with the current.

....

....

....

....

....

....

....

....

....

[Total 6 marks]

Topic P3 — Electricity

Circuit Devices

1 The resistance of a thermistor varies with temperature. (Grade 4-6)

a) Sketch a graph on the axes to show how the resistance of a thermistor changes with temperature.

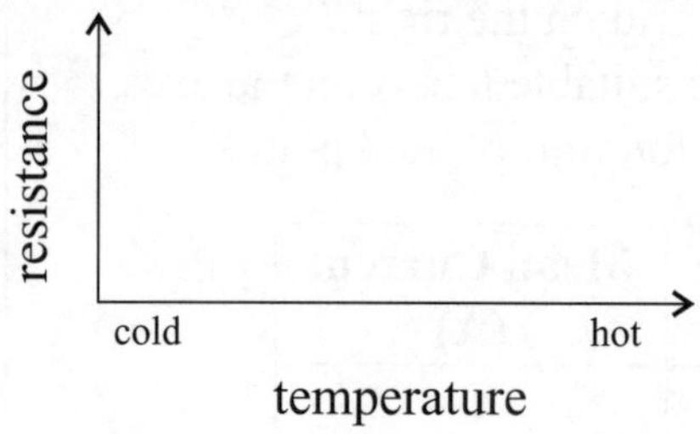

resistance

cold .... hot

temperature

[2]

b) Which is the correct *I-V* graph for a thermistor in constant conditions?

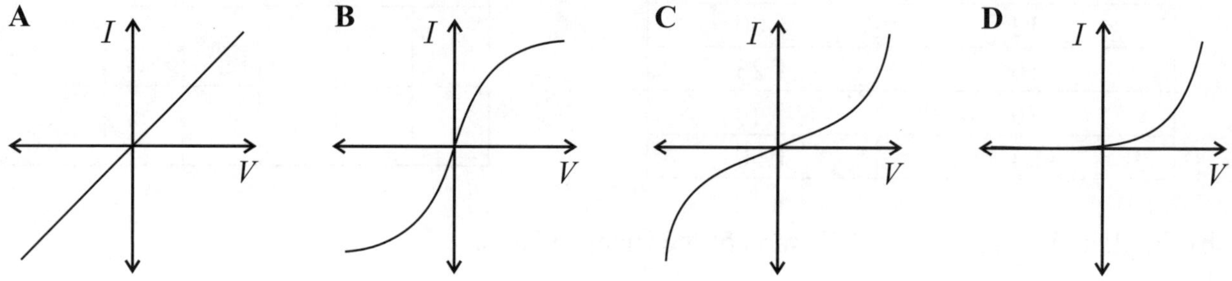

A I / V

B I / V

C I / V

D I / V

Your answer ☐

[1]

[Total 3 marks]

2 Diodes only let current flow in one direction. (Grade 4-6)

a) Why doesn't the current flow in both directions in a diode?

....

[1]

b) Give **one** use of a diode.

....

[1]

[Total 2 marks]

3 The circuit diagram for an automatic night-light in a garden is shown on the right. (Grade 7-9)

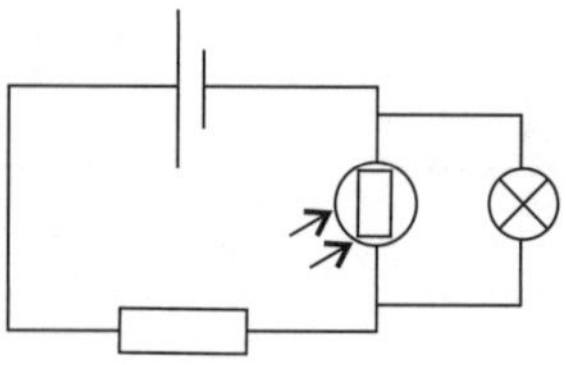

Explain what happens in this circuit as night falls.

....

....

....

....

....

....

[Total 4 marks]

Topic P3 — Electricity

Series and Parallel Circuits

Warm-Up

For the sentences below, state whether they are describing a series circuit, a parallel circuit or both.

Each component can be turned on and off separately. ....

The current through each component is always identical. ....

The potential difference across each component is the same. ....

1 A circuit diagram is shown on the right.

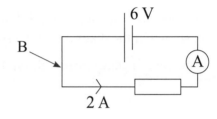

a) Are the components in this circuit connected in series or parallel?

....

[1]

b) What is the current at the ammeter?

Current = ... A

[1]

c) A resistor is added to the circuit at the point marked B. What happens to the ammeter reading?

....

[1]

[Total 3 marks]

2 Two resistors are connected in a circuit with an ammeter, as shown in the diagram on the right.

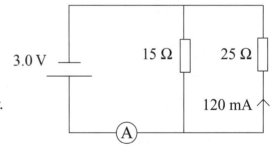

a) Calculate the current flowing through the ammeter.

Current = ... A

[4]

b) Which of the following statements is **true** for the total resistance of this circuit?
   A   Total resistance = 35 Ω
   B   Total resistance = 15 Ω
   C   Total resistance < 15 Ω
   D   Total resistance > 25 Ω

   Your answer ☐

[1]

[Total 5 marks]

Topic P3 — Electricity

42

PRACTICAL

3   Ian is investigating series and parallel circuits, using
     bulbs which are labelled as having the same resistance.
     He sets up the circuit shown in the diagram on the right.

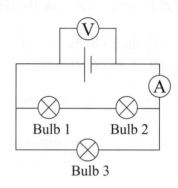

     The voltmeter reads 12 V and the ammeter reads 0.5 A.
     Ian uses these values to calculate the resistance of each bulb.

   a) Calculate the resistance of each bulb.

                                       Resistance =... Ω
                                                                              [2]

   b) i) Ian then adds an identical third bulb in parallel,
           as shown in the diagram on the right.

           Calculate the new current through the ammeter.

                                       Current = ... A
                                                                              [3]

       ii) Ian observes that bulb 3 is brighter than bulbs 1 and 2. Explain why.

       ....

       ....

       ....

       ....

       ....

       ....
                                                                              [5]

   c) Ian now places an ammeter next to bulb 3 and a voltmeter in parallel
       around it, and uses the values to calculate its resistance.
       Why might the resistance differ from the one he calculated earlier?

       ....

       ....
                                                                              [1]
                                                            [Total 11 marks]

Exam Practice Tip

You could be asked to interpret data on any component placed in series or parallel in a circuit. The ideas are the same
though, so try not to panic. Just make sure you really understand how potential difference, current and resistance change.

Topic P3 — Electricity

Energy and Power in Circuits

1 A circuit component has a power of 1.5×10^{-2} kW. *(Grade 4-6)*

a) What is meant by '**power**'?

....

[1]

b) Calculate the energy transferred by the component over 24 hours.

Energy = ... kWh

[2]

[Total 3 marks]

2 If the current through this series circuit doubles, but its total resistance stays the same, what happens to the power of the LED? *(Grade 6-7)*

    A   It halves
    B   It stays the same
    C   It doubles
    D   It quadruples

Your answer ☐

[Total 1 mark]

3 Jane is shopping for a lawn mower. She finds the information in the table online. *(Grade 6-7)*

Lawn Mower	Operating Power
Lawnmagic	920 J per s
Lawn-o-matic	3.24×10^6 J per hr
Bustagrass	1.16 kW

a) Which lawn mower is the most powerful? Show your working.

Lawn mower = ...

[3]

Jane buys the Lawnmagic, and will run it using the mains supply (230 V).
However, the lawn mower needs a fuse fitting in the plug before use.
The fuse used should be rated just a little higher than the operating current of the appliance.

b) Which fuse should Jane fit in the lawn mower plug?

    A   2 A
    B   3 A
    C   5 A
    D   7 A

Your answer ☐

[1]

[Total 4 marks]

Topic P3 — Electricity

Magnets and Magnetic Fields

1 Field lines are used to represent the magnetic field around a magnet.   *Grade 4-6*

a) Which statement is **correct** for magnetic field lines?

  A   They always point from a south pole to a north pole.
  B   They are used to show which direction a charged particle would move in the field.
  C   They can only be straight lines.
  D   They get closer together when the magnetic field is stronger.

  Your answer ☐

  [1]

b) i) Sketch on the diagram the field lines between the poles of these two bar magnets.

  N   **S**

  [2]

  ii) State whether there will be attraction or repulsion between these two poles.

  ....
  [1]
  [Total 4 marks]

2 A student places two metal bars next to each other. One of the bars is a permanent magnet and the other is a magnetic material. She covers both the bars with a piece of paper and scatters iron filings over the top, to show the magnetic field lines around them.   *Grade 6-7*

a) The diagram shows the pattern of the iron filings when they are scattered on the paper.
  Add labels to show the poles on both bars and arrows to the 'field lines' to complete the diagram.

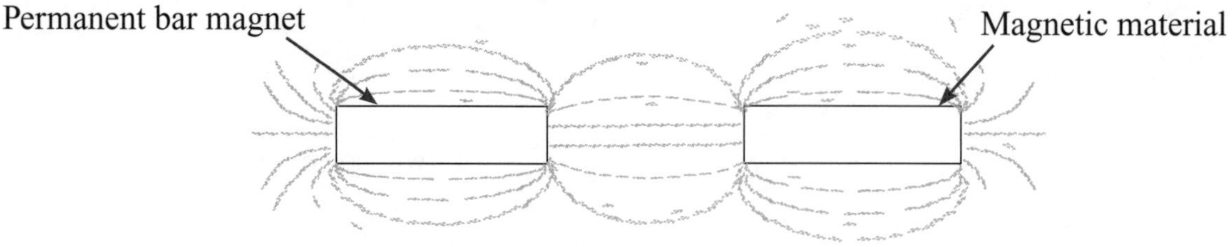

  Permanent bar magnet   Magnetic material

  [3]

b) The permanent magnet is removed and the filings are re-sprinkled above the magnetic material.
  The iron filings no longer show field lines around the magnetic material. Explain why.

  ....

  ....
  [1]

c) Name **one** other piece of equipment that can be used to show field lines.

  ....
  [1]
  [Total 5 marks]

Electromagnetism

1 Sketch a graph on the axes below to show what happens to the magnetic field strength as you get further from a current-carrying wire.

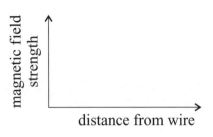

[Total 2 marks]

2 The diagram shows the field lines around a current-carrying wire.

The current through the wire is **decreased**.
Which row correctly describes what happens to the field lines around the wire?

	Distance apart	Direction
A	Increases	Reverses
B	Decreases	Stays the same
C	Decreases	Reverses
D	Increases	Stays the same

Your answer ☐

[Total 1 mark]

3 A current-carrying solenoid has a magnetic field outside it similar to a bar magnet.

a) What happens to the magnetic effect of a solenoid if the number of turns per unit length increases?

....

[1]

b) The north pole of a magnet is brought near to the current-carrying solenoid as shown in the diagram. State whether the north pole is **attracted** or **repelled** by the solenoid. Explain why.

....

....

....

[3]

[Total 4 marks]

Exam Practice Tip

Use your right hand to find the magnetic field direction around a current-carrying wire. Stick your thumb in the direction of the current and curl your fingers — your fingers will be pointing in the direction of the field lines round the wire.

Magnetic Forces

The diagram shows a left hand being used for Fleming's left hand rule.
Using **three** of the labels below, label the thumb and fingers in the diagram.

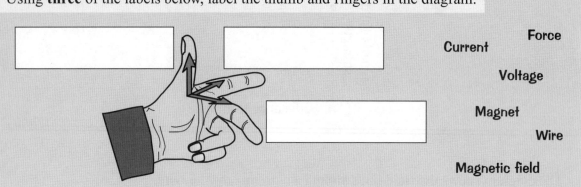

Force
Current
Voltage
Magnet
Wire
Magnetic field

1   How could the force acting on a current-carrying wire in a magnetic field be increased?

A   By decreasing the length of the wire.
B   By decreasing the current through the wire.
C   By reversing the direction of the current.
D   By increasing the strength of the magnetic field.

Your answer ☐

[Total 1 mark]

2   A 30 cm long current-carrying wire is placed between magnetic poles as shown below.

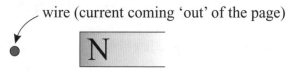

wire (current coming 'out' of the page)

S   •   N

a)   The magnetic flux density is 2.2 T and the current through the wire is 15 A.
Calculate the force acting on the wire. Give the unit.
Use the equation: **Force on a conductor = magnetic flux density × current × length**

Force = ... unit = ...
[3]

b)   Why does the wire experience a force?

....

....

....
[1]

[Total 4 marks]

3 The diagram shows a current-carrying wire between two magnetic poles. A current of 2.6 A is flowing through the wire, from left to right. A force of 0.0183 N is acting on the wire. Its direction is out of the paper, towards you.

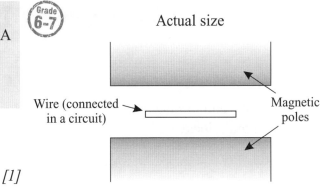

Actual size

Wire (connected in a circuit)

Magnetic poles

a) Label **each pole** to show if it is a north or south pole.

[1]

b) Calculate the magnetic flux density between the poles.
Give your answer to **2** significant figures.
Use the formula: **Force on a conductor = magnetic flux density × current × length**

Magnetic flux density = ... T

[4]

c) The wire is moved so that the current is now running parallel to the magnetic field.
What size force is acting on the wire now?

Force = ... N

[1]

[Total 6 marks]

4 Holly carries out an experiment using a horseshoe magnet and an iron bar connected in a circuit. Part of the set-up is shown below.

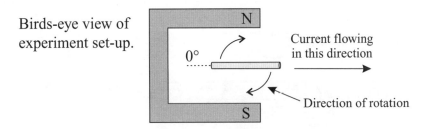

Birds-eye view of experiment set-up.

N

0°

Current flowing in this direction

Direction of rotation

S

Holly rotates the iron bar 90° clockwise and measures the force acting on the bar as she does so. She then plots her results on a graph of force, F, against angle of rotation, θ.

Which of the following graphs shows a sketch of her results?

A
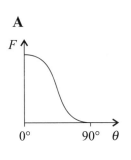

B
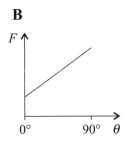

C
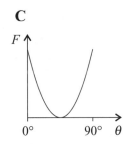

D
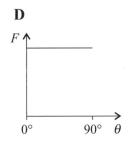

Your answer ☐

[Total 1 mark]

Topic P4 — Magnetism and Magnetic Fields

48

Motors and Loudspeakers

1 The diagram shows a simple motor. *(Grade 6-7)*

a) i) Is the coil turning clockwise or anti-clockwise?

....
[1]

ii) Explain why the coil turns.

....

....

....

....
[3]

b) If the poles of the magnets were swapped round, what effect would this have on the coil's motion?

....
[1]

c) State **two** factors which determine the speed of rotation of a motor.

1. ....

2. ....
[2]

[Total 7 marks]

2 A diagram of a loudspeaker is shown. *(Grade 6-7)*

coil of wire — N — cone
magnets — S

Describe how the loudspeaker uses an alternating current to produce sound.

....

....

....

....

....
[Total 4 marks]

Topic P4 — Magnetism and Magnetic Fields

Electromagnetic Induction

Circle the correct words or phrases below so that the sentences are correct.

Electromagnetic induction is when a <u>potential difference / potential energy</u> is induced in a conductor which is experiencing a change in external <u>electric / magnetic</u> field. If the conductor is part of a <u>complete circuit / open circuit</u>, then a current will flow.

1   Electromagnetic induction can be used to create a current in dynamos and alternators.

a) Which row correctly shows the type of current produced by dynamos and alternators?

	Dynamo	Alternator
A	a.c.	a.c.
B	d.c.	d.c.
C	a.c.	d.c.
D	d.c.	a.c.

Your answer ☐

[1]

b) Give **two** ways you could **decrease** the current produced by an alternator.

1. ....

2. ....

[2]

[3 marks]

2   The diagram below shows the structure of a dynamic microphone.   (Grade 6-7)

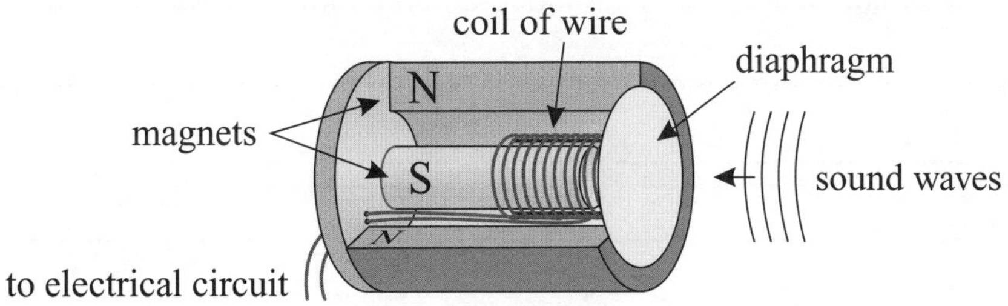

coil of wire

diaphragm

magnets

N

S

sound waves

N

to electrical circuit

Explain how the microphone converts sound waves to electrical signals.

....

....

....

....

....

[Total 4 marks]

3 A wind-up torch contains a dynamo. A handle on the side of the torch is attached to the coil in the dynamo. When the handle is turned, the torch bulb lights up.

Grade 6-7

a) Explain how turning the handle causes the bulb to light up.

....

....

....

[3]

b) Why does turning the handle faster cause the torch light to get brighter?

....

[1]

c) What is the purpose of the split-ring commutator that forms part of the dynamo?

....

[1]

d) The current that the dynamo generates creates its own magnetic field.
Describe the direction that the magnetic field will be created in.

....

[1]

[Total 6 marks]

4 Patryk has set up a simple circuit to measure the current generated when he moves a magnet in and out of a solenoid. A diagram of his set-up is shown.

Grade 7-9

magnet
solenoid
ammeter

a) Will Patryk generate a.c. or d.c. with this set-up?
Explain your answer.

....

....

....

....

[3]

b) Patryk notices the ammeter shows a reading of 0.02 A even when the magnet is still.
How should he deal with this problem?

....

[1]

[Total 4 marks]

> **Exam Practice Tip**
> Remember — for a potential difference to be induced across the ends of a conductor, there must be relative motion between the conductor and an external magnetic field. This one principle is used in both alternators and dynamos.

Topic P4 — Magnetism and Magnetic Fields

Transformers

1 A transformer has 75 turns in the secondary coil.
An input p.d. of 72 V is converted to an output p.d. of 12 V.

  a) Calculate the number of turns on the primary coil. Use the formula:

$$\frac{\textbf{p.d. across primary coil}}{\textbf{p.d. across secondary coil}} = \frac{\textbf{number of turns in primary coil}}{\textbf{number of turns in secondary coil}}$$

Number of turns = ...
[2]

  b) State whether this is a step-up or step-down transformer.

....
[1]

[Total 3 marks]

2 A transformer is made of two coils joined by an iron core.
The primary coil has **twice** the number of turns as the secondary coil.

  a) The input potential difference is 1.6×10^4 V.
What is the output potential difference of this transformer?

  A 8×10^4 V
  B 1.6×10^2 V
  C 8×10^3 V
  D 3.2×10^4 V

  Your answer ☐
[1]

  b) Why **wouldn't** a transformer work if its core was made of wood?

....
[1]

  c) Explain why an alternating current and **not** a direct current is used in transformers.

....

....

....

....
[3]

[Total 5 marks]

Topic P4 — Magnetism and Magnetic Fields

Wave Basics

Add the labels below to the diagram of the wave.

amplitude   crest

rest position

wavelength   trough

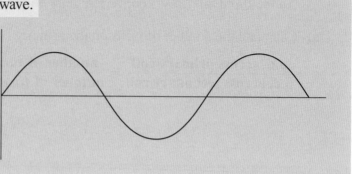

1   Which of the following is **not** a transverse wave?

    A   S waves
    B   light waves
    C   P waves
    D   ripples on the surface of water

Your answer ☐

[Total 1 mark]

2   Waves can be either transverse or longitudinal.

  a) Describe the difference between longitudinal and transverse waves in terms of their vibration and motion.

....

....

....

....

[2]

  b) A transverse wave has a frequency of 1.60×10^4 Hz. Calculate the period of the wave. Give the unit.

Period = ... unit ....

[3]

[Total 5 marks]

3   Which of the following is true for longitudinal waves?

    A   The frequency is the number of compressions plus the number of rarefactions passing a point per second.
    B   They can travel through liquids.
    C   The vibrations are perpendicular to the direction that energy is transferred.
    D   Matter is transferred when they travel through a medium.

Your answer ☐

[Total 1 mark]

4 A child throws a stone into a pond. The stone creates ripples when it hits the water, which spread across the pond.

(Grade 6-7)

a) The ripples pass a leaf floating on the pond.
Explain why the ripples do not carry the leaf to the edge of the pond.

....

....

....

[1]

b) The ripples have a wavelength of 1.5 cm. Given that their frequency is 14 Hz, calculate their speed in m/s. Show your working.

Speed = ... m/s

[3]

[Total 4 marks]

5 A vibrating violin string produces a sound wave.

(Grade 6-7)

A violinist is practising in a village hall. Her teacher sits at the back of the hall to listen.

a) What medium do the sound waves produced by the violin travel through to reach the teacher?

....

[1]

b) The violinist plays a note with a frequency of 2.49 kHz. The sound waves travel at a wave speed of 340 m/s. Calculate the wavelength of the sound waves.
Give your answer to **2** significant figures.

Wavelength = ... m

[4]

c) The violinist then plays a note with a frequency of 220 Hz.
The violinist plays this note for 5.0 seconds.
Calculate how many complete waves are produced by the vibrating string in this time.

Number of waves = ...

[2]

[Total 7 marks]

Topic P5 — Waves in Matter

Wave Experiments

1 A student is investigating water waves in a ripple tank. She sets up the equipment shown below.

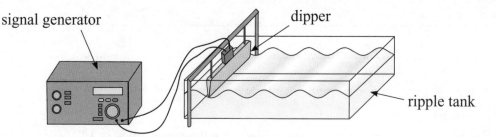

a) The student wants to measure the frequency of the ripples. She floats a cork in the ripple tank and counts how many times it bobs up in 30 seconds. The student repeats her experiment five times. She does not adjust the signal generator between repeats.

State **two** other factors that should remain the same between repeats.

....

....
[2]

b) The table below shows the student's results. She recorded one of the results incorrectly.

Trial	1	2	3	4	5
Number of bobs in 30 seconds	36	33	63	33	42

Calculate the average number of times the cork bobbed up in 30 seconds, ignoring the anomalous result.

Number of bobs = ...
[2]

c) Using your answer to **part b)**, calculate the frequency of the ripples.

Frequency = ... Hz
[1]

d) A second student suggests they could also measure the speed of the ripples. Describe a method they could use.

....

....

....

....

....

....
[3]

[Total 8 marks]

Reflection and Refraction

1 A ray of light meets the boundary between two media. (Grade 4-6)

What is meant by the 'normal' of a boundary?

A   A line at right angles to the boundary.
B   A line parallel to the boundary.
C   A line at right angles to the incident ray at the boundary.
D   A line that represents the boundary.

Your answer [ ]

[Total 1 mark]

2 The diagram below shows light passing from air into a block of glass. The light meets the boundary at an angle of 90°. (Grade 4-6)

Which of the following statements is **correct**?

A   Most of the light will be refracted.
B   Most of the light will be absorbed.
C   Most of the light will be transmitted.
D   Most of the light will be reflected.

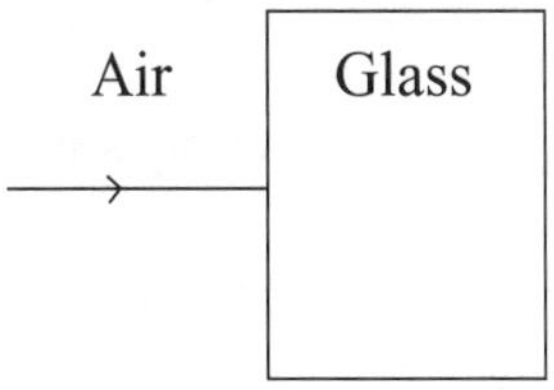

Your answer [ ]

[Total 1 mark]

3 Two rays of light hit a mirror and are reflected. The diagram on the right shows the paths of the two reflected rays. (Grade 6-7)

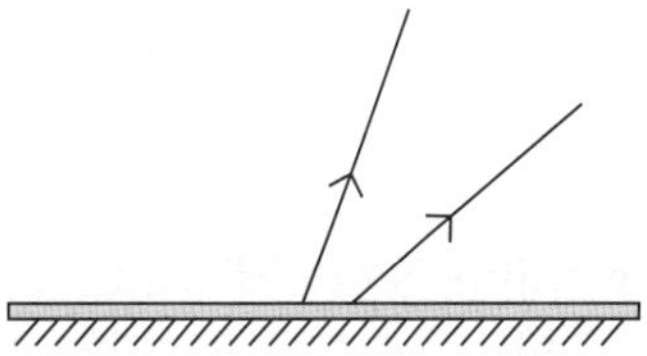

Which diagram below correctly shows the paths of the incident rays?

A

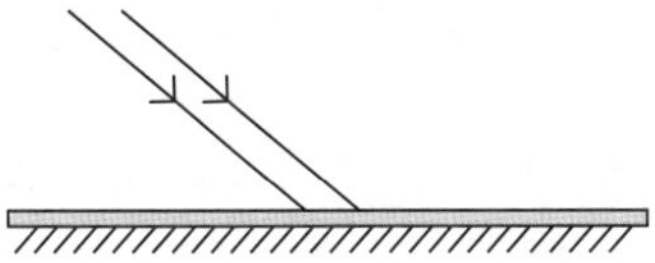

B

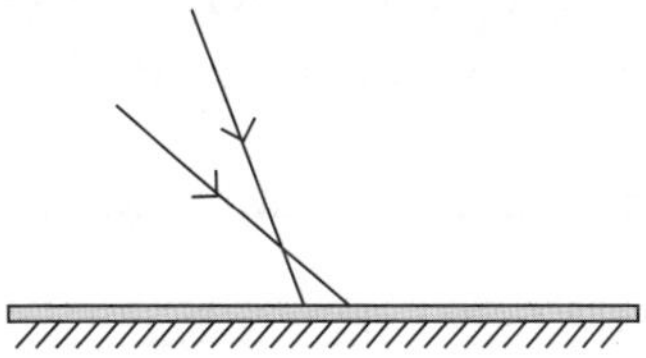

C

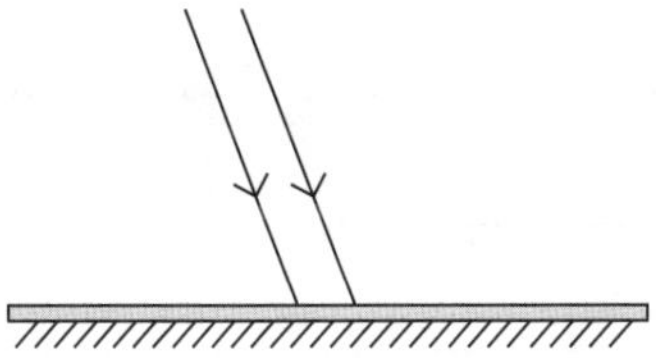

D

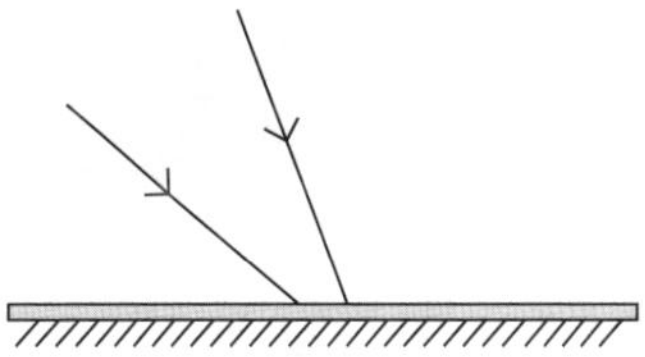

Your answer [ ]

[Total 1 mark]

56

4 A light ray crosses the boundary between two materials, as shown in the diagram on the right.

Grade 6-7

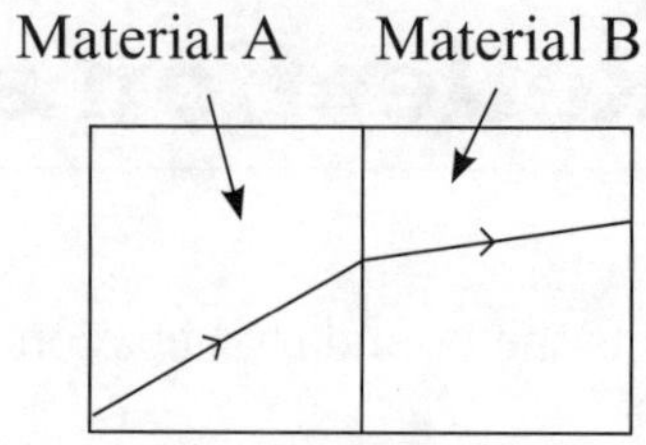

Material A   Material B

a) Material A is less optically dense than material B. How can you tell this from the diagram above?

....

[1]

b) Material B is a type of glass. The light ray passes out of material B into a vacuum.

   i) On the diagram below, sketch the path of the ray as it leaves material B.

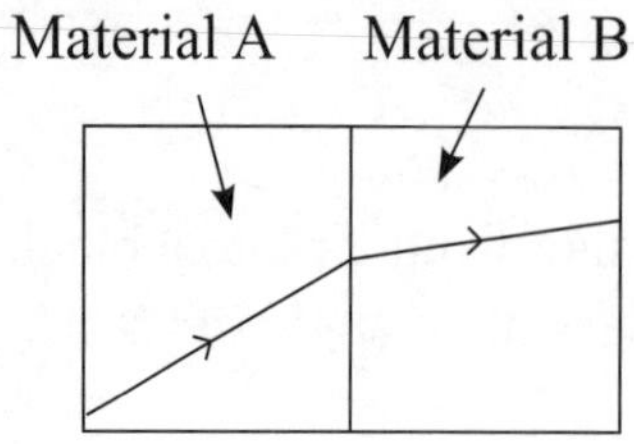

Material A   Material B

[2]

   ii) Explain what happens to the ray's frequency, wavelength and speed as it leaves material B.

....

....

....

....

[4]

[Total 7 marks]

5 A student shines a ray of white light through a block of clear plastic. The path of the light ray is shown on the right.

Grade 7-9

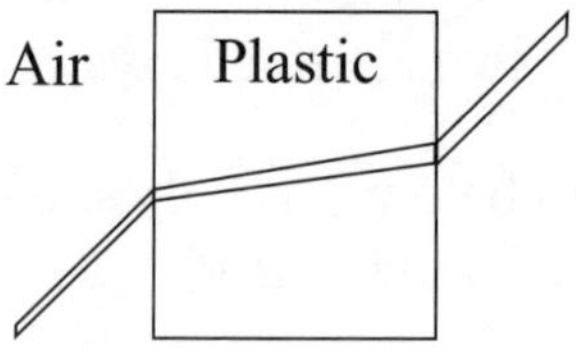

Air   Plastic

The student notices that the emergent ray is not pure white. One side of the emergent ray has a red tinge, whilst the other side looks slightly purple. Explain why this may have happened.

....

....

....

....

....

....

....

[Total 4 marks]

More on Reflection

1   Scott is investigating the reflection of blue light by a mirror.

He places a mirror on a sheet of paper, then draws a normal to the mirror on the sheet of paper. He then shines a ray of blue light towards the point where the normal meets the mirror.

Scott varies the angle between the ray from the light box and the normal, and traces the path of the ray on the paper. He then measures the angle of incidence and the angle of reflection for each ray.

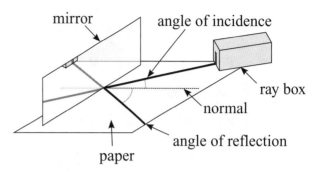

The table below shows Scott's results.

Angle of incidence / °	15	30	45	60	75
Angle of reflection / °	18	33	48	63	78

a) State what kind of error these results show, and suggest what may have caused it.

....

....

[2]

b) Two of Scott's classmates, Jiahui and Francis, do the same experiment. Their results are shown below.

Jiahui's results:

Angle of incidence / °	Angle of reflection / °		
	trial 1	trial 2	trial 3
15	15	14	13
30	31	30	31
45	43	45	44
60	60	61	60
75	74	75	77

Francis' results:

Angle of incidence / °	Angle of reflection / °		
	trial 1	trial 2	trial 3
15	18	12	14
30	33	32	36
45	45	43	49
60	57	64	62
75	70	73	76

Jiahui's results are more repeatable than Francis' results.
Suggest **one** reason for the difference in repeatability of their results.

....

[1]

c) Francis repeats the experiment using red light. Explain how this will affect his results.

....

....

....

[2]

[Total 5 marks]

Topic P5 — Waves in Matter

More on Refraction

Use the words below to correctly fill in the gaps in the passage.
You don't have to use every word, but each word can only be used once.

Different colours of light have .... When they cross a

material boundary, different colours refract .... If you

shine white light through a prism, you get ....

an image   a spectrum   by different amounts   a normal

different speeds in air   by the same amount   a shadow   different wavelengths

PRACTICAL

1 A student wants to investigate the effect of wavelength on how much a ray of light
   refracts when it passes through a glass block. He uses the equipment shown below.

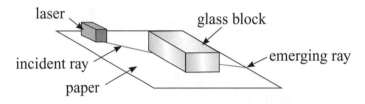

The student shines rays of light with different wavelengths through the glass block.
He traces the path of the incident and emerging rays onto the paper, then joins the two
together to find the path of the refracted ray through the block.
On his diagram, he then measures the angle of incidence and the angle of refraction
for each ray as it enters the block.

a) i) What is the **independent** variable in this experiment?

   ....

   [1]

   ii) What is the **dependent** variable in this experiment?

   ....

   [1]

b) State **two** variables that the student will need to keep the same to make sure
   the experiment is a fair test. Give reasons for your answers.

   ....

   ....

   ....

   ....

   [4]

   [Total 6 marks]

2   You can use ray diagrams to show how light refracts as it passes through different substances.

a) Two parallel rays of light, one red and one blue, are shone on a glass prism, as shown below. The rays are both transmitted by the prism.

On the diagram below, sketch the path taken by the rays through the prism, and when they emerge from the prism.

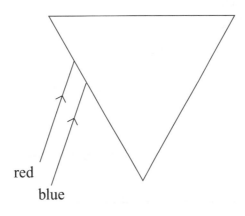

red

blue

[3]

b) A ray of green light from a laser shines on a semicircular glass block. The ray meets the block at the centre of its straight side, as shown below, and is transmitted into the block.

On the diagram below, sketch the path taken by the ray through the glass block, and when it emerges from the block.

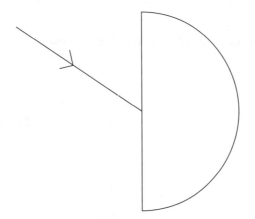

[2]

[Total 5 marks]

Exam Practice Tip

Remember, for any question that asks you to draw a ray diagram, you should always draw in a dotted normal to any boundary the ray meets before you start. This makes it a lot easier to judge whether your ray is going along the normal or at an angle to it, so you can figure out what will happen to the ray.

Topic P5 — Waves in Matter

Sound Waves and Hearing

1 The range of human hearing is 20-20 000 Hz.

a) On the diagram below, which label shows the part of the ear which converts vibrations to electrical signals?

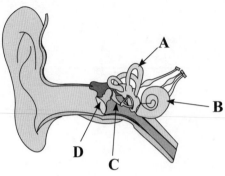

Your answer ☐

[1]

b) Explain why humans can only hear sounds over a limited range of frequencies.

....

....

....

[1]

[Total 2 marks]

2* A woman is listening to music being played by a stereo. Explain how vibrations of the speaker lead to the woman being able to hear the music, from the point where the speaker vibrates to the point where the woman perceives a sound.

....

....

....

....

....

....

....

....

....

[Total 6 marks]

Topic P5 — Waves in Matter

Sonar and Ultrasound

1   A doctor is treating a patient who she suspects may have a kidney infection.   **Grade 6-7**

The doctor decides to take an ultrasound image of the patient's kidneys.

a) Explain how ultrasound can be used to produce images of structures in the body like the kidneys.

....

....

....

....

....

....

....

[4]

b) As well as medical imaging, ultrasound waves are also used in sonar by ships and submarines. Give **one** other use of ultrasound waves.

....

[1]

[Total 5 marks]

2   A military ship is using sonar to patrol for submarines.   **Grade 7-9**

a) The ship sends out an ultrasound wave and detects a reflected pulse 1.04 s later. The speed of sound in seawater is 1500 m/s.

Given that the depth of the seabed in the area is known to be 1600 m, state whether this suggests that there may be a submarine beneath the ship. You **must** support your answer with a calculation.

....

....

[3]

b) Suggest **one** way that submarines could make themselves less visible to sonar. Give a reason for your answer.

....

....

....

[2]

[Total 5 marks]

EM Waves and Their Uses

Using the words in the box, put the waves of the electromagnetic spectrum in the table below, in order of frequency.

low frequency						→ high frequency
....	....	....	....	....	....	....
....	....	....	....	....	....	....

microwaves   ultra-violet   visible light   gamma rays

infra-red   X-rays   radio waves

1 Which of the following is a type of ionising radiation? *Grade 4-6*

    A   ultra-violet
    B   microwaves
    C   visible light
    D   infra-red

Your answer [ ]

[Total 1 mark]

2 Which of these statements about the electromagnetic spectrum is **not** true? *Grade 4-6*

    A   All electromagnetic waves travel at the same speed in a vacuum.
    B   The longer the wavelength of an electromagnetic wave, the more energy it carries.
    C   Our eyes can only detect a small part of the electromagnetic spectrum.
    D   Electromagnetic waves transfer energy from a source to an absorber.

Your answer [ ]

[Total 1 mark]

3 Radio waves have the longest wavelengths in the electromagnetic spectrum. Gamma rays have the shortest. *Grade 4-6*

a) Radio waves are used to broadcast TV and radio shows. Give **one** other use of radio waves.

....

[1]

b) Give **one** use of gamma rays.

....

[1]

[Total 2 marks]

4 A naturalist uses a night vision camera to capture an image of a fox, as shown below.

Explain how the night vision camera allowed this image to be taken.

....

....

....

....

[Total 2 marks]

5 X-rays are used in hospitals to diagnose broken bones.

The X-rays are generated by accelerating electrons to high speeds then firing them at a metal plate. When the electrons hit the plate, X-rays are produced.

a) Explain how these X-rays can be used to generate an image of a bone.

....

....

....

....

....

....

[3]

b) Staff who work with X-ray machines wear badges that monitor the levels of radiation they have been exposed to.

Explain why it is important to make sure hospital staff are exposed to as little X-ray radiation as possible.

....

....

....

....

[2]

[Total 5 marks]

64

6 Microwaves and visible light can both be used to transmit telephone calls. (Grade 6-7)

a) Explain how visible light is used to transmit phone signals.

....

....

....

....

[2]

b) Land-line calls are usually transmitted using visible light.
However, microwaves are sometimes used to transmit long-distance calls via satellites.

Suggest **one** advantage to using microwaves rather than
light waves to transmit phone signals over long distances.

....

....

[1]

c) Radio waves are also used in communications.
Which row on the table below correctly describes the conditions needed to generate radio waves?

	Changing electric field?	Changing magnetic field?
A	no	no
B	no	yes
C	yes	no
D	yes	yes

Your answer ☐

[1]

[Total 4 marks]

7 Researchers are currently investigating if it would be possible to send humans to Mars.
One of the concerns would be the increased risk of cancer. (Grade 7-9)

Suggest and explain **one** possible reason for this increased risk.

....

....

....

....

....

[Total 3 marks]

Waves in Medical Imaging

1 X-rays can be used to generate X-ray photographs and CT scans. *Grade 4-6*

a) The image below shows an X-ray photograph of a hand. Which of these statements is correct?

    A   The darker the image, the more the
          X-rays have been absorbed by the hand.

    B   The lighter the image, the more the
          X-rays have been transmitted by the hand.

    C   The lighter the image, the more the
          X-rays have been absorbed by the hand.

    D   The darker the image, the more the
          X-rays have been reflected by the hand.

Your answer ☐

[1]

b) Give **one advantage** and **one disadvantage** of CT scans compared to ultrasound scans.

Advantage: ....

Disadvantage: ....

[2]

[Total 3 marks]

2 Simone has been researching the different types of waves used in medical imaging. *Grade 6-7*

The table below shows her results.

Type of wave	Ionising?	How it works
ultrasound	yes	Waves are reflected from boundaries between tissues.
X-rays	yes	Waves are absorbed and transmitted differently by different tissues.
infra-red	no	Waves are reflected by areas of infected tissue.

a) Simone has made **two** mistakes. What are they?

....

....

[2]

b) Simone says that X-rays are dangerous, so they shouldn't be used in medical imaging.
Explain the extent to which you agree with Simone's statement.

....

....

....

....

....

[3]

[Total 5 marks]

3 Infra-red cameras can be used in airports to check if any passengers have a fever. *Grade 6-7*

a) Explain how an infra-red camera can be used to check for a fever.

....

....

....

....

[2]

b) Suggest **one** advantage of checking for fevers with an infra-red camera instead of a thermometer.

....

[1]

[Total 3 marks]

4 Gamma rays can be used to detect cancerous tumours. *Grade 6-7*

a) Explain how gamma rays can be used to detect cancer.

....

....

....

....

....

....

....

....

[4]

b) Ultrasound waves can also be used to detect tumours.

i) Give **one** advantage of using gamma rays to detect tumours instead of ultrasound waves.

....

....

[1]

ii) Give **one** advantage of using ultrasound waves to detect tumours instead of gamma rays.

....

[1]

[Total 6 marks]

Exam Practice Tip

Hopefully you'll have noticed by now, but the uses (and dangers) of all the waves you've met so far come down to how they're absorbed, transmitted, reflected and emitted from different substances, and the energy they carry. If you ever have to compare the uses of different waves, think about these aspects of their behaviour and you won't go far wrong.

Topic P5 — Waves in Matter

Visible Light and Colour

1 Which row in the table below correctly shows three colours of light in order of increasing frequency?

	— increasing frequency →		
A	red	blue	green
B	yellow	red	violet
C	blue	green	yellow
D	orange	green	violet

Your answer ☐

[Total 1 mark]

2 A student is investigating the effect of coloured filters on the appearance of different objects.

The student sets up the equipment below, then blocks out all other sources of light in the room.

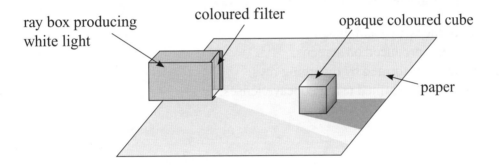

a) The student places a white cube on the paper and a red filter in front of the ray box.
State the colour that the cube appears.

....
[1]

b) The student replaces the white cube with a blue one.
What colour does the cube appear now? Explain your answer.

....

....

....

....
[3]

c) State what would happen if the student were to add a blue filter to the ray box,
in front of the red filter.

....
[1]

[Total 5 marks]

Topic P5 — Waves in Matter

Lenses and Images

Draw lines to connect each statement to the correct lens.

Usually called a convex lens.

Usually called a concave lens.

Also known as a diverging lens.

Also known as a converging lens.

Brings parallel rays together to a point.

Spreads parallel rays out.

1 Which of the following statements is **not** true? Grade 4-6

A   A mirror produces a virtual image.
B   Real images are produced on screens.
C   Virtual images are formed by diverging rays.
D   Real images can be formed using concave lenses.

Your answer ☐

[Total 1 mark]

2 A student uses a concave lens to create an image of a match. Grade 7-9

Complete the ray diagram below to show how an image is formed by the lens.

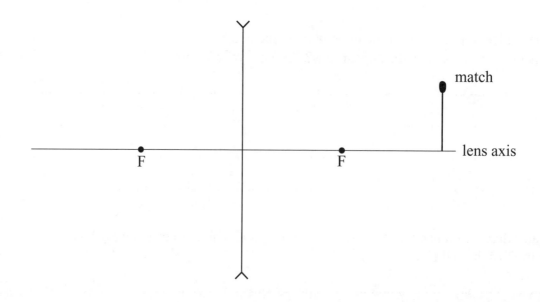

match

F   F   lens axis

[Total 3 marks]

 ☐   ☐   ☐

More on Lenses

1 Long-sightedness can be corrected using lenses. (Grade 6-7)

a) Explain why the image appears blurry when a long-sighted person tries to focus on a near object.

....

....

....
[2]

b) Explain how lenses can correct long-sightedness.

....

....

....

....
[3]

[Total 5 marks]

2 A student uses a convex lens to create an image of a pencil. (Grade 7-9)

a) Complete the ray diagram below to show how an image is formed by the lens.

2F   F   B   F   2F   lens axis

[4]

b) The pencil is moved to the point marked B on the diagram above. Describe how the image of the pencil will change. Include the new position of the image in your answer.

....

....

....

....
[4]

[Total 8 marks]

Topic P5 — Waves in Matter

Isotopes and Radioactive Decay

The standard notation used to represent atoms is shown. Use the words below to correctly fill in the labels. You don't have to use every phrase, but each phrase can only be used once.

$$_{Z}^{A}X$$

electron number

neutron number

mass number

chemical symbol

charge   atomic number

1 One isotope of sodium is $_{11}^{23}$Na. *(Grade 4-6)*

a) i) How many protons are in a sodium nucleus?

....

[1]

ii) Calculate the number of neutrons in the sodium nucleus.

Number of neutrons = ...

[1]

b) Describe what is meant by the term isotope.

....

....

[2]

[Total 4 marks]

2 Unstable isotopes can emit nuclear radiation, such as alpha particles. *(Grade 4-6)*

a) What is an alpha particle made up of?

A   Two neutrons and two protons.
B   An electron.
C   Gamma rays.
D   Four neutrons and two protons.

Your answer ☐

[1]

b) Some isotopes will emit an electromagnetic wave as well as an alpha particle. Name the wave. Give its charge and mass.

Name: ....

Charge: .... Mass: ....

[3]

[Total 4 marks]

Radiation Properties and Decay Equations

1   A polonium nucleus, $^{210}_{84}\text{Po}$, can occasionally decay to a lead nucleus (Pb) by releasing alpha and gamma radiation. Write a balanced equation to show this decay.

....

[Total 3 marks]

2   Anandi carries out an experiment to investigate two different radioactive sources. A setup of her experiment is shown. She changes the material between the source and the Geiger-Muller tube and measures the count rate. A table of her results is also shown.

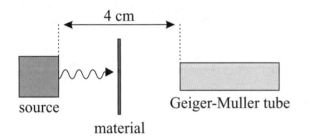

Material	Count rate (counts per minute)	
	Source A	Source B
No material	854	1203
Paper	7	1200
Aluminium	6	8
Lead	6	7

a) What happens to the mass and charge of the nuclei of source A when they decay?

....

....

[2]

b) Source B is an isotope of carbon (C), which has a mass number of 14 and an atomic number of 6. The carbon nuclei decay to nitrogen (N) nuclei. Write a balanced equation to show this decay.

....

[4]

c) Anandi removes the material and moves source B from **4 cm** to **1 m** away from the detector. Explain what will happen to the count rate as she moves the source.

....

....

....

[2]

[Total 8 marks]

Exam Practice Tip

You need to know how the penetration properties of alpha, beta and gamma radiation differ — gamma radiation has the longest range in air and alpha radiation has the shortest. Beta radiation sits somewhere in-between.

Electron Energy Levels

Use the words in the box to correctly fill in the gaps in the passage.
You don't have to use every word, but each word can only be used once.

absorb

ionised

excited

release

energy

frequency

The electrons around an atom sit in different .... levels, or shells.

An electron is said to be .... when it moves up an energy level.

An electron that falls back down an energy level will .... radiation.

---

1 An alpha particle collides with a neutral atom, as shown in the diagram below. **Grade 4-6**

a) Complete the sentence:

The atom has now become...

A   ... neutralised.
B   ... ionised.
C   ... contaminated.
D   ... a beta particle.

nucleus

electrons

after
alpha particle
collides

Before

After

Your answer ☐

[1]

b) What kind of **charge** does the atom have after the collision?

....

[1]

[Total 2 marks]

---

2 A fluorescent tube light contains mercury vapour and has a phosphor coating on the inside. When the light is on, electrons in the atoms of the mercury are excited, which results in them emitting UV radiation. This radiation is absorbed by atoms in the phosphor coating, causing them to emit visible light. **Grade 7-9**

a) Explain why the mercury atoms release radiation.

....

....

[2]

b) Why do the mercury atoms and the atoms in the phosphor coating emit different forms of electromagnetic radiation?

....

....

....

[3]

[Total 5 marks]

Half-Life

1 The half-life of a radioactive source can be found from an activity-time graph like the one shown below.

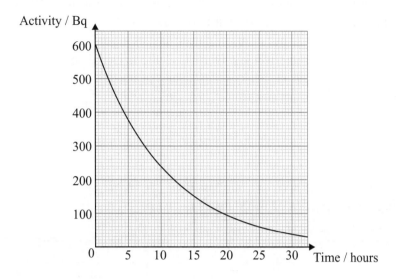

a) Define the term half-life.

....

[1]

b) Use the graph to determine the half-life of the source.

Half-life = ... hours
[1]

c) A different source with a half-life of 300 minutes has an initial activity of 400 Bq. Show how its activity will change in the first 20 hours on the graph above.

[3]

[Total 5 marks]

2 A radioactive source initially has an activity of 6000 Bq.

a) After 6 years, the source has an activity of 750 Bq. What is the half-life of the source?

Half-life = ... Unit ....
[3]

b) A sample of the same source has an initial activity of 64 Bq. Calculate the net decline in activity, expressed as a ratio, during radioactive emission after 2 half-lives for this source.

Ratio = ...
[3]

[Total 6 marks]

Topic P6 — Radioactivity

Dangers of Radioactivity

1 Which of the following statements is **true**? (Grade 4-6)

    A   Contamination and irradiation only last as long as the original source is present.

    B   Contamination is temporary, but irradiation lasts longer.

    C   Irradiation is temporary, but contamination lasts longer.

    D   Contamination and irradiation last even after the original source has been removed.

Your answer ☐

[Total 1 mark]

2 Rebekah is looking at the radioactive sources they use in her lab. A table showing the properties of the sources is given. (Grade 6-7)

Source	Radiation Emitted	Form
A	Alpha	Solid
B	Alpha and gamma	Gas
C	Gamma	Gas

a) Which source poses the greatest risk to those using it? Explain your answer.

....

....

....

....

[3]

Rebekah writes out some safe handling instructions for the lab.

Safety precautions for working with radioactive sources
• Always wear gloves when working with radioactive sources.
• Keep sources as close to you as possible at all times.
• Use tongs to handle any solid radioactive material.
• Place sources in a lead lined box when not in use.

She has made **one** mistake.

b) Circle the incorrect statement. Why is this statement incorrect?

....

....

....

[3]

[Total 6 marks]

Half-Life and Uses of Radiation

1   The table below outlines some properties of four radioactive materials.

Which would be the best source to use as a tracer?

	Type of radiation emitted	Half-life
A	Gamma	6 hours
B	Beta	500 years
C	Alpha	4 hours
D	Gamma	70 years

Your answer ☐

[Total 1 mark]

2   Two sources, X and Y, emit the same type of radiation and initially have the same number of radioactive nuclei. Source X has a half-life of 24 hours and source Y has a half-life of 10 years.

Which source is the **safest** to be around? Explain your answer.

....

....
[Total 2 marks]

3   A patient is receiving cancer treatment. They undergo a procedure to have a beta-emitting implant placed next to their tumour. In a few months, they will have the implant removed.

a) Explain why a beta-emitting source is used for the implant.

....

....

....
[2]

b) Why will the implant be removed after a few months?

....

....
[1]
[Total 3 marks]

Topic P6 — Radioactivity

4* A tumour in the body can be treated using an external gamma radiation source. Explain the process involved.

Grade 6-7

....

....

....

....

....

....

....

....

....

....

[Total 6 marks]

5 Sources of radiation can be used in medical imaging to explore internal organs. Iodine-123 is a radioactive isotope that is absorbed by the thyroid. Grave's disease causes an overactive thyroid, so the thyroid will absorb more iodine than usual.

Grade 7-9

a) Briefly explain how iodine-123 could be used to determine if a patient has Grave's disease.

....

....

....

....

....

[3]

b) Iodine-123 emits gamma radiation. Why wouldn't an alpha emitter be used for medical imaging?

....

....

[2]

[Total 5 marks]

Exam Practice Tip

Ionising radiation can cause cells to mutate and divide uncontrollably. But it can also be used to kill cancerous cells. You need to understand how this is done with radiotherapy, including why different types of radiation are used.

Fission and Fusion

For the sentences below, state whether they are describing nuclear fission, nuclear fusion or both.

It can happen spontaneously. ....

It is the main source of energy for stars. ....

It releases energy, which is carried away by radiation. ....

It can start when a nucleus absorbs a neutron. ....

It usually involves large and unstable nuclei. ....

It usually involves light nuclei. ....

1   Nuclear fission is one method of generating electricity. (Grade 4-6)

a)   What is nuclear fission?

....

....

[1]

b)   Outline how the absorption of a neutron by a uranium nucleus can lead to a chain reaction.

....

....

....

....

....

[4]

[Total 5 marks]

2   Nuclear fusion releases energy. (Grade 6-7)

a)   What is nuclear fusion?

....

[1]

b)   Which of the following statements about nuclear fusion is **correct**?

A   total mass of nuclei before nuclear fusion = total mass of nuclei after nuclear fusion
B   total mass of nuclei before nuclear fusion > total mass of nuclei after nuclear fusion
C   total mass of nuclei before nuclear fusion < total mass of nuclei after nuclear fusion
D   total mass of nuclei before nuclear fusion ∝ total mass of nuclei after nuclear fusion

Your answer ☐

[1]

[Total 2 marks]

Conservation of Energy

For each example, name the energy store that energy is being transferred away from.

1) A skydiver falling from an aeroplane. ....

2) A substance undergoing a nuclear reaction. ....

3) A stretched rubber band springing back to its original shape. ....

4) A piece of burning coal. ....

1 A kettle of cold water is plugged into the mains and brought to the boil. Energy is transferred from the mains to the water. *Grade 4-6*

a) Name the energy store of the water that the energy is transferred **to**.

....

[1]

b) How is energy transferred from the mains to the kettle?

A mechanically
B by heating
C by radiation
D electrically

Your answer ☐

[1]

c) i) State the law of conservation of energy.

....

....

[2]

ii) Assuming the kettle is a closed system, describe the change in total energy that takes place as the water boils.

....

[1]

[Total 5 marks]

2 Sonja is riding her bike. She takes her feet off the pedals to freewheel down a hill. *Grade 6-7*

Describe the energy transfers that take place as the bike travels down the hill. Ignore friction and air resistance.

....

....

....

[Total 3 marks]

Efficiency

1 Which of the following washing machines is the most efficient?

Washing machine	Input energy (J)	Useful output energy (J)
A	4×10^4	2.52×10^4
B	4×10^4	2.80×10^4
C	4×10^4	2.95×10^4
D	4×10^4	2.98×10^4

Your answer ☐

[Total 1 mark]

2 An electric fan transfers 7250 J of energy. 2 kJ of this is wasted energy.

a) Suggest **one** way in which energy is wasted by the fan.

....

[1]

b) Calculate the efficiency of the fan. Give your answer as a decimal to **2** significant figures.

Efficiency = ...

[4]

[Total 5 marks]

3 An electric kettle has an efficiency of 76%. 2500 J of energy is transferred from the mains to the kettle every second. When the kettle is full, it needs to transfer 418 000 J of energy to the thermal energy store of the water to boil it.

How long does a full kettle need to be switched on for in order to boil the water?

A 2.8 minutes
B 22 seconds
C 167 seconds
D 220 seconds

Your answer ☐

[Total 1 mark]

Exam Practice Tip

No device is 100% efficient as some energy will always be wasted. For example, energy is carried away by sound waves — you can probably hear an electrical appliance in your home if it's turned on, even if it's just a quiet hum.

Topic P7 — Energy

Energy Transfer by Heating

1 Water in a bucket heats up by conduction and convection when a lump of hot coal is put in it. *(Grade 4-6)*

a) Explain how energy is transferred through the water by conduction, causing its temperature to rise.

....

....

....

....

....

[4]

b) Another lump of hot coal is buried under some sand. Why doesn't the sand heat up by convection?

....

[1]

[Total 5 marks]

2 A matt black pan full of hot water is left to cool in a room. The initial temperature of the water is 85°C and after 30 minutes it has cooled down to 43°C. The water loses 441 000 J of energy in this time. The specific heat capacity of water is 4200 J/kg °C. *(Grade 6-7)*

a) Calculate the mass of water in the pan. Show your working. Use the formula:
change in thermal energy = mass × specific heat capacity × change in temperature

Mass = ... kg

[3]

b) i) Energy is transferred away from the surface of the **pan** in **three** ways. Name them.

1. ....

2. ....

3. ....

[3]

ii) Explain why the **pan** would cool down at a slower rate if it was shiny and silver in colour.

....

....

....

[2]

[Total 8 marks]

Reducing Unwanted Energy Transfers

1 Randeesh is cycling in a race. Before the race, he puts oil on the bike chain. **Grade 4-6**

Explain, using ideas about energy, how adding oil will affect the efficiency of Randeesh's cycling.

....

....

....

....

[Total 4 marks]

2 Camilla is building an energy-efficient house. **Grade 6-7**

She has four brick brands to choose from for the walls.

Brand	Thermal conductivity (m²/s)	Brick thickness (cm)
A	5.2×10^{-7}	10
B	5.2×10^{-7}	15
C	2.7×10^{-7}	10
D	2.7×10^{-7}	15

a) Based on the information in the table above, explain which brick brand she should use.

....

....

....

....

[4]

b)* Describe **other ways** that Camilla could make her house energy-efficient.
   Include how each of your suggestions reduce energy losses.

....

....

....

....

....

....

....

....

[6]

[Total 10 marks]

Mechanical and Electrical Energy Transfers

Use the words below to correctly fill in the gaps in the passage.
You don't have to use every word, and words can be used more than once.

As a rubber ball falls, it experiences .... due to gravity.

.... is done on the ball and energy is transferred from the ball's

.... energy store to its .... energy store.

The ball compresses when it hits the ground. Energy is transferred from the ball's

.... energy store to its .... energy store.

a force	work	chemical potential	kinetic
elastic potential	radiation	gravitational potential	friction

1 An electric heater with a power rating of 3 kW is connected to the mains. *(Grade 4-6)*

a) Which statement correctly describes the energy transfer occurring when the heater is switched on?
   A Energy is transferred electrically to the kinetic energy store of the heater.
   B Energy is transferred by heating to the kinetic energy store of the heater.
   C Energy is transferred electrically to the thermal energy store of the heater.
   D Energy is transferred by heating to the thermal energy store of the heater.

   Your answer ☐
   [1]

b) What is meant by the power rating of an appliance?

   ....
   [1]

c) The heater is on for 5 hours. How much work is done by the mains in that time?
   Use the formula: **energy transferred = power × time**. Give the unit.

   Work done = ... unit = ...
   [2]
   [Total 4 marks]

2 A 0.1 kg toy contains a compressed spring. When the spring *(Grade 4-6)* is released, the toy flies 0.5 m upwards from ground level.

Calculate the energy stored in the toy's gravitational potential energy store at its highest point.

Energy = ... J
[Total 3 marks]

3 Dylan is investigating the speed at which a light foam ball (9×10^{-3} kg), dropped from up to 2 m, hits the floor. He plans to use a 30 cm ruler to record the initial height of the ball and a light gate connected to a computer to find the final velocity.

Grade 6-7

His teacher tells him that the ruler is inappropriate for this experiment.

a) Give **one** reason why. Suggest equipment he could use instead of the ruler.

....

....

[2]

Dylan's results are shown in the table.

Height (m)	Attempt 1 (m/s)	Attempt 2 (m/s)	Attempt 3 (m/s)	Mean Speed (m/s)
0.5	3.06	3.08	3.10	3.08
1.0	4.27	4.36	4.31	4.31
1.5	5.10	5.12	5.08	5.10
2.0	5.96	5.98	6.01	

b) i) Complete the table by calculating the missing value.

[1]

ii) Explain the trend shown by the data in terms of the transfer of energy between different stores.

....

....

....

....

....

[3]

c) i) Using the idea of energy transfers, calculate the speed at which the ball should hit the floor from a height of **5 m**. Use: gravitational field strength (g) = 10 N/kg.

Speed = ... m/s

[4]

ii) Dylan measures the speed of the ball dropped from 5 m and finds it to be **lower** than that calculated in **c) i)**. Suggest why.

....

....

....

[2]

[Total 12 marks]

Topic P7 — Energy

4 An empty lift has a mass of 1150 kg. The lift always moves at the same steady speed between each floor, and the distance between each floor is 4.00 m. *Grade 7-9*

a) How much energy is transferred to the lift's gravitational potential energy store when it moves from the second floor to the sixth floor? Use: $g = 10$ N/kg.

    A 1.84×10^5 J
    B   18.4 kJ
    C   46 000 kJ
    D 4.6×10^3 J

Your answer ☐

[1]

b) A motor is used to move the lift. The lift takes 10.0 s to move up four floors. Calculate the power of the motor if it has an efficiency of 0.80.

Power = ... W
[3]

[Total 4 marks]

5 Amy and Ben fire identical 10.0 g ball bearings from different catapults. The rubber band of each catapult is elastically extended by 0.100 m and then released to fire the ball bearings. *Grade 7-9*

a) The rubber band in Ben's catapult has a spring constant of **1.44 N/cm**. How much energy is transferred to the kinetic energy store of Ben's ball bearing? Use the formula: **energy transferred in stretching = 0.5 × spring constant × (extension)²**

    A   0.0072 J
    B   0.072 J
    C   0.72 J
    D   7.2 J

Your answer ☐

[1]

b) The initial speed of Amy's ball bearing is twice as fast as Ben's ball bearing. Calculate the spring constant of Amy's rubber band. Show your working.

Spring constant = ... N/m
[5]

[Total 6 marks]

Exam Practice Tip

A tricky few pages here, but it's not really as bad as it seems. Just make sure you learn the equations for power and for calculating kinetic, gravitational potential and elastic potential energy store values. Then it's just a matter of working out how the energy is being transferred between the different stores and whether there's any energy being wasted or not.

Everyday Speeds and Accelerations

1 What is the approximate speed of a pedestrian walking down a quiet street? *Grade 4-6*

    A   15 m/s

    B   1.4 m/s

    C   3.0 m/s

    D   13 m/s

Your answer ☐

[Total 1 mark]

2 A train is travelling at 95 mph. *Grade 6-7*

What is the speed of the train in m/s?

    A   15 m/s

    B   210 m/s

    C   42 m/s

    D   26 m/s

Your answer ☐

[Total 1 mark]

3 A cyclist is travelling along a main road. *Grade 6-7*

a) The cyclist is wearing a helmet which contains a layer of foam covered in plastic.
Explain how the foam in the helmet would help to protect the cyclist in the event of a crash.

....

....

....

....

....

[3]

b) The cyclist stops at a red light. When the light changes to green, the cyclist rides away,
accelerating up to a speed of 21 km/hr.

Estimate the cyclist's acceleration. Give your answer in **m/s²**.

Acceleration = ... m/s²

[4]

[Total 7 marks]

Reaction Times and Stopping Safely

Warm-Up

Use the words below to correctly fill in the gaps in the passage.
You don't have to use every word, but each word can only be used once.

The .... distance of a vehicle is made up of the thinking distance

and the .... distance. The braking distance of a car is ....

if the car is heavily loaded and if conditions are ....

A vehicle is more likely to skid if its tyres are ....

shallower	shorter	thinking	stopping
braking	icy	bald
longer	noisy	distracting	deeper

1 A student is measuring their reaction time using a computer program. (Grade 4-6)

a) What is a typical value for a person's reaction time?

A 500 milliseconds
B 50 seconds
C 50 milliseconds
D 5 seconds

Your answer ☐

[1]

b) The student presses the enter key on the computer keyboard to start the program.
After a random time interval, the computer sounds a buzzer. The student presses the enter key
again as soon as they hear the buzzer. The computer then calculates their reaction time.

Describe how the computer might calculate the student's reaction time.

....

....

[1]

c) The student repeats the experiment three times and calculates an average reaction time.

Explain why this is done.

....

....

[1]

[Total 3 marks]

Topic P8 — Global Challenges

2 A car is travelling at 30 mph (13 m/s) along a road in dry conditions. (Grade 6-7)

a) Which is the best estimate of the car's stopping distance?

A 2.5×10^2 m
B 25 m
C 0.1 km
D 9 m

Your answer ☐

[1]

b) The car **doubles** its speed, but all other factors remain the same.

i) How does this affect the driver's thinking distance?

....

[1]

ii) Explain how this affects the car's braking distance.

....

....

[2]
[Total 4 marks]

3* A group of friends are driving home from a concert late at night. (Grade 6-7)
It is raining heavily and they are listening to loud music on the radio.

Describe the factors that could affect the car's stopping distance on this journey.
Explain the effect each factor could have.

....

....

....

....

....

....

....

....

....

....

....

[Total 6 marks]

88

4 A car of mass 1000 kg is travelling at a speed of 18 m/s. A deer jumps out in front of the car, so the driver performs an emergency stop. The brakes of the car exert a force of 6000 N.

a) The work done by the brakes to stop the car is equal to the energy in the kinetic energy store of the car before braking. Calculate the car's braking distance. Show your working.

Distance = ... m

[4]

b) The driver's reaction time is 0.5 s. Calculate the overall stopping distance of the car.

Distance = ... m

[2]

c) The driver avoids the deer, and continues to the airport, where he picks up four passengers and their luggage. This increases the weight of the car by 30%. The car is travelling back at 18 m/s when a second deer jumps out in front of it. Given that the force exerted by the brakes is still 6000 N, calculate the deceleration of the car. Give your answer to **2** significant figures.

Deceleration = ... m/s²

[4]

[Total 10 marks]

5 A car manufacturer tests the brakes of a new model of car.

The car is driven at a steady speed of 15 m/s in dry conditions.
The driver applies the brakes when told to. The velocity-time graph of the test is shown below.

On the same axes, sketch the graph you would expect if the test was repeated at the same speed, with the same driver, but in **wet** conditions.
Assume the driver is told to stop at the same time in both tests.

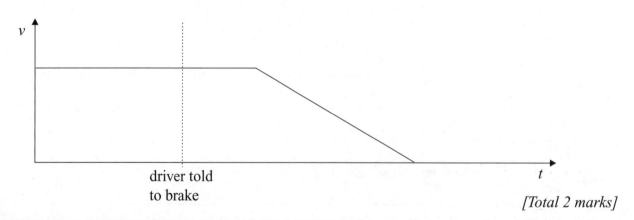

[Total 2 marks]

Exam Practice Tip

You need to be neat, even if you're just sketching a graph — the examiner needs to see what you're trying to show. Remember to use a pencil, so you can correct any mistakes, and if you're drawing a straight line use a ruler.

Topic P8 — Global Challenges

Energy Sources

1 Which row **only** lists sources that release carbon dioxide when used to generate electricity?

	Energy Sources
A	oil, uranium, coal
B	uranium, gas, hydro-electricity
C	wind, hydro-electricity, oil
D	oil, gas, coal

Your answer ☐

[Total 1 mark]

2 Nuclear power stations use non-renewable nuclear fuel to generate electricity.

a) Which of the following is a **renewable** energy source?

    A   oil

    B   gas

    C   tides

    D   plutonium

Your answer ☐

[1]

b) Briefly describe how a nuclear power station generates electricity.

....

....

....

[3]

c) Give **two** disadvantages of nuclear power.

....

....

[2]

[Total 6 marks]

3 The amount of electricity generated by wind turbines is increasing in the UK.

a) How do wind turbines generate electricity?

....

....

[2]

b) Why might people want to increase the amount of electricity generated by wind turbines?

....

....

[2]

[Total 4 marks]

Topic P8 — Global Challenges

4 Electricity can be generated by burning bio-fuels, such as animal waste collected from farms or specially grown crops like sugar cane. (Grade 6-7)

a) Are bio-fuels a renewable or non-renewable energy source? Explain your answer.

....

....

[2]

b) Suggest **one advantage** and **one disadvantage** of growing crops for use as bio-fuel compared to burning waste.

Advantage:...

....

....

Disadvantage: ....

....

....

[2]

[Total 4 marks]

5 A sunny coastal country is debating replacing a coal-fired power station with a different form of electricity generation. (Grade 6-7)

a) Give **three** reasons why the country might want to stop using coal as a source of energy.

....

....

....

....

[3]

b) Suggest **two** sensible replacement energy sources for this country. Compare their use to coal.

....

....

....

....

....

....

....

[5]

[Total 8 marks]

Topic P8 — Global Challenges

6 The bar chart below shows the electricity generated from renewable and non-renewable energy sources in a small country over 20 years.

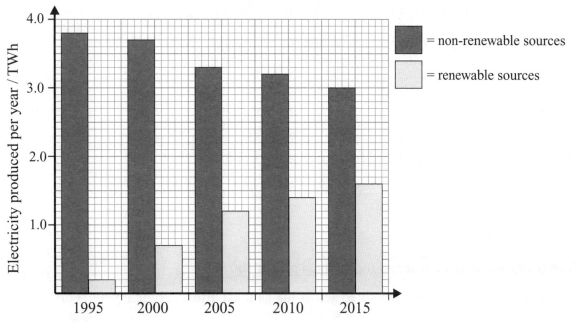

a) How much electricity did the country produce from renewable sources in 2005?

.... TWh

[1]

b) i) How much **more** electricity did the country produce per year in 2015 than in 1995?

.... TWh

[2]

ii) Suggest **one** reason why the country needed to produce more electricity.

....

[1]

c) Describe the trends in use of energy sources shown by the graph.
Suggest reasons for these trends. Use data from the graph in your answer.

....

....

....

....

....

....

....

....

[4]

[Total 8 marks]

Topic P8 — Global Challenges

Electricity and the National Grid

1 Electricity is supplied to homes in the UK through the national grid. **Grade 4-6**

a) The electricity supply of the UK has an alternating voltage. What does this mean?

....

....

[1]

b) State the potential difference and frequency of the UK mains electricity.

....

[1]

[Total 2 marks]

2 Electricity is transmitted across the national grid at 400 000 V. **Grade 6-7**

a) Explain why electricity is transmitted across the national grid at a high potential difference.

....

....

....

....

....

....

[3]

b) The diagram on the right shows a transformer at a sub-station. It changes the potential difference generated by a wind farm from 12 000 V to 400 000 V.

primary coil:
12 000 V
300 A

secondary coil:
400 000 V
? A

i) Calculate the current in the secondary coil of the transformer. Use the formula:

$$\textbf{potential difference across primary coil} \times \textbf{current in primary coil} = \textbf{potential difference across secondary coil} \times \textbf{current in secondary coil}$$

Current = ... A

[2]

ii) Explain whether this is a step-up or step-down transformer.

....

....

[1]

[Total 6 marks]

Topic P8 — Global Challenges

Wiring in the Home

Warm-Up

Draw lines to match the type of wire to its colour in a typical plug.

LIVE WIRE   EARTH WIRE   NEUTRAL WIRE

blue   brown   green and yellow

1   Explain why touching the live wire in a socket is dangerous. (Grade 4-6)

....

....

....

[Total 2 marks]

2   Metal kettles in the UK include an earth wire for safety. (Grade 6-7)

  a) State the potential difference between the earth wire and the live wire in a socket.

....

[1]

  b) Explain what would happen if you touched the earth wire in a normally functioning kettle.

....

....

....

[2]

  c) A metal kettle develops a fault and the live wire inside it touches the metal casing.
      Explain how the earth wire and the fuse act to keep the kettle safe when it is switched on.

....

....

....

....

....

[3]

[Total 6 marks]

Topic P8 — Global Challenges

The Solar System and Orbits

Complete the diagram below by writing in the names of the planets.
Three have been done for you.

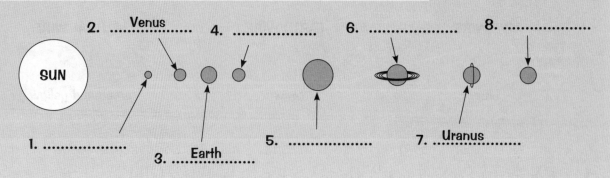

1   What kind of object is Pluto?   Grade 4-6

    A   a planet
    B   a natural satellite
    C   an artificial satellite
    D   a minor planet

Your answer ☐

[Total 1 mark]

2   What force keeps the Moon in orbit around the Earth?   Grade 4-6

    A   electrostatic
    B   nuclear
    C   gravitational
    D   magnetic

Your answer ☐

[Total 1 mark]

3   The diagram shows the paths of four satellites orbiting Earth.
Which satellite is the most suitable one for monitoring the weather?   Grade 6-7

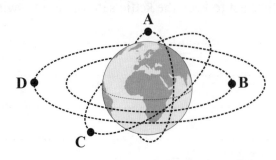

Your answer ☐

[Total 1 mark]

4 A communications network launches a satellite for transmitting telephone signals. **Grade 6-7**

a) State the kind of orbit the satellite should have.

....

[1]

b) Explain why this orbit is suitable for transmitting telephone signals.

....

....

....

[2]

c) The satellite is now in orbit around the Earth, receiving and transmitting phone signals.

i) What evidence is there to show that there is a force acting on the satellite?

....

....

....

....

....

[3]

ii) In what direction is this force acting?

....

[1]

[Total 7 marks]

5 A planet has two identical natural satellites with stable orbits, as shown below. **Grade 7-9**

Which satellite is travelling faster, X or Y? Explain your answer.

....

....

....

....

[Total 3 marks]

The Origin of the Universe

1   The table shows a list of galaxies and their distance from Earth in light years.

Galaxy	Distance From Earth (light years)
Cigar Galaxy	12 million
Black Eye Galaxy	24 million
Sunflower Galaxy	37 million
Tadpole Galaxy	420 million

The light from the galaxies in the table shows red-shift.

a) i) Describe what is meant by red-shift.

....

....

....
[2]

ii) Light from which of the galaxies in the table will show the greatest red-shift?
Explain your answer.

....

....

....
[3]

b) i) Explain how the red-shift of light from distant
galaxies provides evidence for the Big Bang model.

....

....

....

....

....

....

....
[4]

ii) Name **one** other piece of evidence that supports the Big Bang model.

....
[1]

[Total 10 marks]

The Life Cycle of Stars

1 The diagram below shows the life cycle of a star. **Grade 4-6**

Protostar   Main sequence star   X   White dwarf

What is the name of the life cycle stage marked X?

A   neutron star
B   red supergiant
C   red dwarf
D   red giant

Your answer [ ]

[Total 1 mark]

2* Betelgeuse is a star which is much more massive than our Sun. **Grade 6-7**

Describe the life cycle of a massive star like Betelgeuse, beginning from a cloud of dust and gas.

....

....

....

....

....

....

....

....

....

....

[Total 6 marks]

Exam Practice Tip

This is just one of those areas of physics where you need to learn a lot of words and facts I'm afraid. So make sure you can remember all the stages in the life cycle of a star and in particular how our own Sun was formed.

Topic P8 — Global Challenges

Emitting and Absorbing Radiation

1 A cake is removed from the oven and left to cool to room temperature. **Grade 4-6**

When the cake is at room temperature, which of the following statements is correct?

A   The cake absorbs more radiation than it emits.
B   The cake emits more radiation than it absorbs.
C   The cake no longer emits or absorbs radiation.
D   The cake emits the same amount of radiation as it absorbs.

Your answer ☐

[Total 1 mark]

2 Explain why the temperature of a can of cold drink increases when it's placed on a table in a warm room. **Grade 4-6**

....

....

....

[Total 2 marks]

3 The graphs on the right show how atmospheric carbon dioxide concentration and temperature have changed over time. **Grade 7-9**

a) Explain the link between atmospheric carbon dioxide and the Earth's temperature.

....

....

....

....

[2]

b) Isaac states 'These graphs prove that an increased atmospheric carbon dioxide level causes global warming.' Use the graphs and your ideas about correlation and cause to evaluate his statement.

....

....

....

....

....

....

[5]

[Total 7 marks]

4   Star A is a red giant with a temperature of 4000 °C and
     Star B is a main sequence star with a temperature of 5500 °C.

a) Which graph shows the intensity-wavelength distribution of the stars?

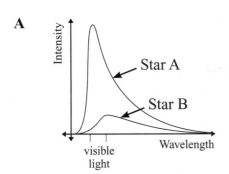

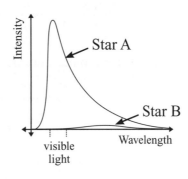

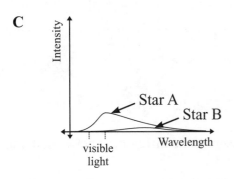

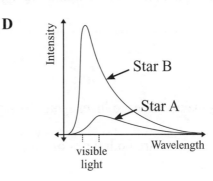

Your answer ☐

[1]

b) Use your knowledge of intensity and wavelength distribution to explain why some objects glow red when they are heated.

....

....

....

....

....

....

[4]

[Total 5 marks]

Exam Practice Tip

Examiners love asking questions where you have to apply your physics knowledge to everyday, real-life situations.
They're not just being mean, that's why you study physics — it has real-life applications. Don't panic when it happens
— just go over what you do know in your head, and then see how it works in the situation they've described.

Sonar and Seismic Waves

1   Sonar can be used by ships and submarines to measure the depth of the seabed.   Grade 4-6

a) What kind of waves does sonar use?

....

[1]

b) Explain how sonar is used to measure the depth of the seabed.

....

....

....

....

....

....

[3]

[Total 4 marks]

2   We can use seismic waves to investigate the structure of the Earth.   Grade 6-7

a) S waves and P waves are both types of seismic wave. Describe the differences between them.

....

....

....

[3]

The graph below shows how the velocity of a P wave changes as it travels through the Earth.

Velocity (km/s)

Depth (km)

X-

Y-

MANTLE

OUTER CORE

INNER CORE

b) Explain why the velocity of the wave suddenly changes at depth X and Y.

....

....

....

....

[3]

[Total 6 marks]

Mixed Questions

1   A scientist is carrying out an experiment to find the specific heat capacity
     of water. A sketch of her experiment and her results are given below.

She heats 0.64 kg of water in a large grey sealed box using a 336.0 W electric heater. The heater
is on for 120.0 s and she records the temperature of the water before and after this time.

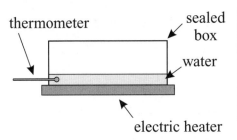

Attempt	Temperature before (°C)	Temperature after (°C)	Change in temperature (°C)
1	19.0	33.6	14.6
2	22.2	37.8	
3	25.7	40.5	14.8
	Mean change in temperature		

a) Fill in the **two** missing values in the table.

                                                                                          [2]

b) Assuming there are no energy losses, calculate the energy
    transferred to the water by the electric heater.

                                                   Energy transferred = ... J
                                                                                          [2]

c) Find the specific heat capacity of the water and give the unit. Use the formula:
    change in thermal energy = mass × specific heat capacity × change in temperature

                          Specific heat capacity = ... Unit ....
                                                                                          [3]

d) The specific heat capacity of water is actually lower than the value calculated by the student.
    What colour container should the student have used to make her results more accurate?
    A   silver
    B   maroon
    C   black
    D   brown
    Your answer ☐   [1]

e) The student now heats the water to 100 °C, causing all the water to boil and become water vapour.
    Explain what will happen to the pressure inside the box as the temperature rises above 100 °C.

....

....

....
                                                                                          [3]
                                                                             [Total 11 marks]

2 Sophie is having trouble reading the text in her workbook. She claims that the paper causes specular reflection of light, which makes the writing look blurry.

a) Why is Sophie wrong?

....

[1]

It turns out that Sophie is long-sighted and must wear glasses.

b) Complete the ray diagram below to show the image of the workbook page being formed by one lens of her glasses.

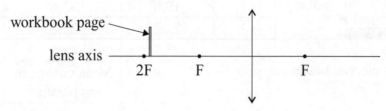

[3]

c) Each lens of her glasses has a volume of 2.12 cm³ and the frames have a mass of 5.00 g. If the density of glass is 2.70 g/cm³, calculate the total mass of her glasses. Show your working. Give your answer to **3** significant figures.

Mass = ... g

[4]

[Total 8 marks]

3 X-rays and gamma rays are types of electromagnetic waves.

a) What is the frequency of an X-ray travelling at 3×10^8 m/s with a wavelength of 4.8×10^{-9} m?

A 1.60×10^{16} Hz
B 1.25×10^{16} Hz
C 6.25×10^{16} Hz
D 1.44×10^{16} Hz

Your answer ☐

[1]

b) State **one** use of each of the following electromagnetic waves.

X-ray: ....

Gamma ray: ....

[2]

c) The equation shows a nucleus emitting a gamma ray. State what values A and B should be.

$$^{202}_{81}\text{Tl} \rightarrow\ ^{A}_{81}\text{Tl} + ^{B}_{0}\gamma$$

A = ...   B = ...

[2]

[Total 5 marks]

Mixed Questions

4   The diagram shows a solenoid with a current flowing through it.
Five points mark where a compass has been placed.

axis through
centre of
solenoid

1

4

2

3

5

current in

current out

a) Which two points will have the compass needle pointing in the same direction?

A   1 and 2
B   1 and 4
C   2 and 5
D   3 and 5

Your answer ☐

[1]

b) The solenoid is connected in series with a 12.0 V power supply. A current of 3.20 A
flows through the solenoid. Calculate the resistance of the wire of the solenoid.

Resistance = ... Ω
[3]
[Total 4 marks]

5   Sam is using a radiation detector to investigate two different radioactive sources.

a) The count rate of source A drops from 7640 counts per minute to 1910 counts per minute in
1.5 hours. Find the half-life of the source. Give your answer in **minutes**.

Half-life = ... mins
[2]

b) When Sam puts a thin sheet of aluminium in front of the detector, the count rate of source A
drops significantly. Name the **two** types of radiation that the source could be emitting.

....
[2]

Source B is an alpha-emitter. An alpha particle is the same
as the nucleus of the most common isotope of helium.

c) State the mass number of the most common isotope of helium.

....
[1]
[Total 5 marks]

Mixed Questions

6 Cars A and B take part in a straight line drag race. They both set off at the same time and both engines provide a force of 5.6 kN to the cars throughout the race. The cars both reach terminal velocity before slowing down at the end.

a) The two cars are identical apart from their shape. Car B is more streamlined than car A. Which of the following is **true**?

    A   Car A will reach its terminal velocity first.
    B   Both cars will reach their terminal velocity at the same time.
    C   Car B will reach its terminal velocity first.
    D   Both cars slow down as they reach their terminal velocity.

Your answer ☐

[1]

b) Car A has an initial acceleration of 3.5 m/s².
Calculate its mass, ignoring air resistance and friction.

Mass = ... kg
[3]
[Total 4 marks]

7 The diagram shows the pressure acting on the outside of a boat when it is stationary and floating in a lake.

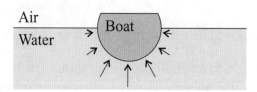

a) Explain why the arrows are different sizes.

....

....

....
[3]

b) The speed of sound in water is 1480 m/s. If it takes 158 ms for a sound wave to travel from the surface of the lake to the bed, how deep is the lake? Give your answer to **3** significant figures.

Depth = ... m
[3]
[Total 6 marks]

8   An electric hob has four separate rings. One ring is used to heat a pan of water.   (Grade 6-7)

a) The ring has an input voltage of 230 V and a current of 6.0 A through it.
What is its power?

   A   1.38 kW
   B   13.8 kW
   C   38.3 kW
   D   2.76 kW

Your answer ☐

[1]

b) i) For every 2200 J of energy transferred to the hob, 1496 J of energy is transferred
to the thermal energy store of the water. Calculate the efficiency of the hob.
(You can assume the pan conducts energy perfectly and is 100% efficient.)

Efficiency = ...

[2]

ii) Suggest how energy is **lost** from the system.

....

....

[1]

c) The water in the pan requires 24 288 J of energy to increase its temperature from 18 °C to 22 °C.
Calculate how long the ring needs to be on for to increase the temperature by this much.
Give your answer to **2** significant figures.

Time = ... s

[4]

d) i) The four rings of the hob are all connected in parallel to the mains supply.
Describe **two** advantages of connecting the rings in parallel.

....

....

[2]

ii) One of the rings has a **lower** resistance than the other three. How will the amount
of current flowing through it differ to the current flowing through the other rings?

....

[1]

[Total 11 marks]

Mixed Questions

9 Oona is investigating how the compression of a spring affects the velocity of a trolley. She sets up her experiment as shown below. She pushes the trolley to compress the spring. Then she releases the trolley and measures its velocity as it passes through the light gate. She repeats the experiment, altering the amount of compression each time.

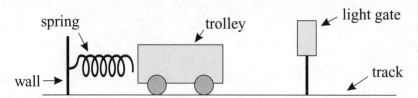

a) i) State the **independent** and **dependent** variables in this experiment.

Independent variable: ....

Dependent variable: ....

[2]

ii) Suggest **two** things Oona should do to make this a fair test.

....

....

[2]

b) The trolley has a weight of 8.80 N. What is its mass? Use: $g = 10$ N/kg.

   A 8.8×10^1 kg
   B 8.8×10^{-1} kg
   C 8.8×10^{-2} g
   D   0.0088 kg

Your answer ☐

[1]

When the spring was compressed by 0.0400 m,
the trolley's velocity was 0.600 m/s at the light gate.

c) i) Ignoring friction and air resistance, calculate the spring constant of the spring. Use the formula: **energy transferred in stretching = 0.5 × spring constant × (extension)²**

Spring constant = ... N/m
[4]

ii) The spring constant of the spring is actually higher than the value calculated in **c) i)**. Explain why.

....

....

....

[2]

[Total 11 marks]

Mixed Questions

10   The national grid uses pylons, transformers and cables to
     transfer energy electrically from power stations to consumers.

The ratio of the number of turns in a transformer's primary coil to the number of turns in its secondary coil is 1:2. You can assume that the transformer is 100% efficient.

a) i) If the input voltage of the transformer is 13 500 V, calculate its output voltage.
       Use the formula:
$$\frac{\text{p.d. across primary coil}}{\text{p.d. across secondary coil}} = \frac{\text{number of turns in primary coil}}{\text{number of turns in secondary coil}}$$

Output voltage = ... V

[2]

ii) Which row correctly states the effect the transformer will have on the output current and power?

	Current	Power
A	Halves	No change
B	Halves	Doubles
C	Doubles	No change
D	Doubles	Doubles

Your answer ☐

[1]

The energy transfers that take place in most power stations are quite similar. It's mainly the source energy store that differs.

b)* Compare how a coal power station and a nuclear power station work, including a description of the energy transfers that take place.

....

....

....

....

....

....

....

....

[6]

[Total 9 marks]

Mixed Questions

PRACTICAL

11 Louise wants to investigate how the potential difference across a diode varies with current.

a) Draw a circuit diagram to show how Louise should set up her circuit.

[4]

The results of her experiment are shown in the table.

Setting	Current / A				Potential difference / V			
	Repeat 1	Repeat 2	Repeat 3	Mean	Repeat 1	Repeat 2	Repeat 3	Mean
A	0.31	0.33	0.31		0.26	0.23	0.23	0.24
B	0.46	0.61	0.44	0.45	0.53	0.51	0.51	0.52
C	0.57	0.59	0.59	0.58	1.40	1.02	1.00	
D	0.60	0.62	0.61	0.61	1.52	1.47	1.48	1.49

b) i) Calculate the **two** missing values.

[2]

   ii) Calculate the work done by the diode if the circuit is left on for 13.2 s on setting B.
       Give your answer to **2** significant figures and state the unit.

Work done = ... Unit ....

[4]

c) Use your knowledge of the expected I-V graph of a diode to comment on Louise's results and any mistakes she might have made.

....

....

....

....

[3]

Diodes can be used to convert alternating current into direct current.

d) Sketch a graph on the axes to show a cathode ray oscilloscope trace of an alternating current of 10 V.

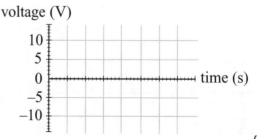

[2]

[Total 15 marks]

12 The diagram shows a Van de Graaff generator which is used to generate a positive charge on a metal dome.

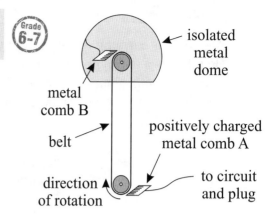

The Van de Graaff generator consists of a metal dome and a belt made of insulating material wrapped round two wheels. The wheels turn in order to turn the belt.

The bottom of the belt continuously brushes past metal comb A, which is positively charged. The top of the belt continuously brushes past metal comb B, which is attached to the metal dome.

a) Explain how a charge builds up on the dome.

....

....

....

....

....

....

[5]

b) Explain why the metal dome of a Van de Graaff generator is not connected to an earth wire.

....

....

[2]

An earthed piece of metal is brought near to the charged dome.

c) i) Explain what you'd expect to happen now.

....

....

[2]

ii) Just before the metal was brought close, a charge of 15 µC had built up on the dome and the potential difference between the dome and the earthed piece of metal was 320 kV. Calculate the energy transferred away from the dome during the event described in c) i). Show your working.

Energy = ... J

[4]

[Total 13 marks]

Mixed Questions

PRACTICAL

13   A student is carrying out an experiment to find the frictional force acting on a trolley.
He releases a trolley from a marked position at the top of a ramp. The trolley rolls
down the ramp, along a horizontal track and then up a second ramp at the other side.
The diagram below shows the experimental setup.

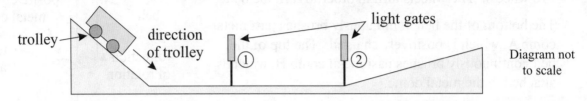

a) i) The table shows his results. Fill in the final column in the table.

Repeat	Speed at light gate 1 (m/s)	Speed at light gate 2 (m/s)	Time taken to travel between light gates 1 and 2 (s)	Acceleration (m/s²)
1	1.22	0.76	2.00	
2	1.16	0.62	2.25	
3	1.19	0.75	2.00	

[3]

ii) The mass of the trolley is 300 g. Use information in the table to calculate
the **magnitude** of the frictional force acting on the trolley.

Force = ... N

[4]

b) Complete the free body force
diagram to show the forces
acting on the trolley when it's
moving along the horizontal
part of the track.

direction of
motion

⟶

[3]

The student sticks sandpaper onto the horizontal part of the track and repeats the experiment.

c) What effect will the sandpaper have on the height reached by the trolley on the second ramp?
Explain your answer.

....

....

....

....

....

....

[5]

[Total 15 marks]

Mixed Questions

14   Telescopes are used in astronomy to detect various forms of electromagnetic radiation.

A standard light telescope uses refraction to form an image.

a) i)   Complete the ray diagram to show the two rays of orange light being brought to focus.

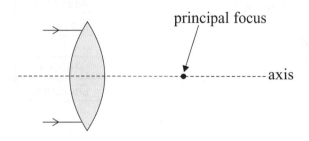

[4]

ii) The top ray in the diagram above is replaced with a ray of indigo light. It enters the lens in exactly the same plane and at the same angle as the original orange ray.
Show, on the same diagram, how this indigo ray would be refracted through the lens.

[3]

A telescope that detects infra-red radiation is mounted on a satellite that has a stable geostationary orbit round the Earth.

b) i)   Which of the following statements about the orbit of the satellite is **correct**?

A   The speed of the satellite is always changing.
B   One complete orbit takes 12 hours.
C   The orbital radius increases with each orbit.
D   The force acting on the satellite is due to gravity.

Your answer [ ]

[1]

ii) Suggest why the telescope is placed in space, and not on the Earth.

....

....

....

[2]

c)   The telescope is super-chilled to keep its temperature really low.

Use your knowledge of the intensity-wavelength distribution of everyday objects to explain why this telescope needs to operate at a low temperature.

....

....

....

....

....

[4]

[Total 14 marks]

15   Christine is playing with some marbles in the lab.

Two of her marbles have the same volume (4.2×10^{-6} m³), but are made of different materials. Marble A is made of rubber. She isn't sure what marble B is made of.

She finds the following table in a textbook.

a) What is the mass of marble A?

Material	Average density (g/cm³)
Porcelain	2.30
Glass	2.70
Rubber	1.21
Diamond	3.53

   A 5.08×10^{-3} kg
   B 5.08×10^{3} kg
   C 5.08×10^{-3} g
   D   0.000508 kg

Your answer ☐

[1]

Christine balances the two marbles on a plank that is pivoted at its centre, as shown below.

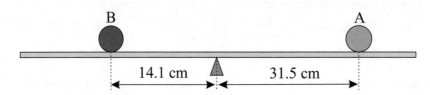

B   A

14.1 cm   31.5 cm

b) Marble B is made of one of the four materials listed in the table above.
   What is marble B made of? Show your working. Use: gravitational field strength (g) = 10 N/kg.

Material of marble B = ...

[6]

Christine rolls two new marbles, C and D, towards each other and they collide.
After the collision, both marbles have a different momentum. The diagram shows the velocities and masses of both marbles before the collision. (You can ignore friction and air resistance.)

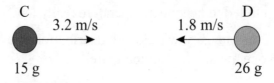

C   3.2 m/s   1.8 m/s   D

15 g   26 g

c) What will happen when the marbles collide?

   A   They will both move off together towards the left.
   B   They will both move off together towards the right.
   C   Marble C will move to the left and marble D will come to a stop.
   D   They will both come to a stop.

Your answer ☐

[1]

[Total 8 marks]

Mixed Questions